Sarah Skinner Dunn

Webster University

NOAH
and the
GOLDEN TURTLE
Stories from the East and West for the ESL Student

PRENTICE-HALL, INC.   Englewood Cliffs, New Jersey 07632

Library of Congress Cataloging in Publication Data

DUNN, SARAH SKINNER.
   Noah and the golden turtle.

   Bibliography: p.
   1. English language—Text-books for foreign speakers.
2. Readers—East and West.   3. Religions—Fiction.
4. Tales. I. Title.
PE1128.D844 1985   428.6'4   84-11324
ISBN 0-13-622945-X

Editorial/production supervision and
interior design: Chrystena Chrzanowski
Cover design: George Cornell
Manufacturing buyer: Harry P. Baisley

Printed in the United States of America

10 9 8 7 6 5 4 3 2 1

ISBN 0-13-622945-X   01

PRENTICE-HALL INTERNATIONAL, INC., *London*
PRENTICE-HALL OF AUSTRALIA PTY. LIMITED, *Sydney*
EDITORA PRENTICE-HALL DO BRASIL, LTDA., *Rio de Janeiro*
PRENTICE-HALL CANADA INC., *Toronto*
PRENTICE-HALL OF INDIA PRIVATE LIMITED, *New Delhi*
PRENTICE-HALL OF JAPAN, INC., *Tokyo*
PRENTICE-HALL OF SOUTHEAST ASIA PTE. LTD., *Singapore*
WHITEHALL BOOKS LIMITED, *Wellington, New Zealand*

For Robert, Eliza, Katie, Christie, and Bobby

Contents

Preface

Noah and the Golden Turtle: Stories from the East and West for the ESL Student is designed for high-intermediate ESL students. The theoretical rationale for the reading text is based upon Schumann's acculturation model for second-language acquisition and Smith and Goodman's psycholinguistic model for reading.

According to John Schumann's model, cultural differences can play a major role in limiting the total second-language ability of a learner. He addresses these limitations from the point of view of the function of language, dividing it into three components: communicative, integrative, and expressive.

Through the communicative function information is exchanged among persons. The integrative function serves to mark one's identity within society and the expressive function is designed to allow the expression of certain psychological needs. (1974, p. 140)

Initially, second-language learners use language only in its communicative function. The second language at this stage is characterized by its simplification and reduction. When students' needs develop beyond simple communication to integration into the society of the second language, their language skills must improve to allow acculturation to take place. For many students this is not an easy point to reach, for it requires, to a certain extent, a rejection of their own language. Richard Rodriguez, in *A Memoir of A Bilingual Child*, expresses this experience of rejection. "For my part, I felt that by learning English I had somehow committed a sin of betrayal." (1981, p. 36) Such rejection is perceived as similar to a loss of identity.

Schumann also attributes this reluctance on the part of the second-language learner to social and psychological factors that increase the distance between the learner and speakers of the target language. One of the factors affecting this distance is the attitude of each group toward the other. "If both groups positively value each other, these favorable views will be communicated to the learner and will enhance his acquisition of the target language." (1978, p. 79) A way to communicate favorable views is to show an awareness of and an appreciation for students' cultural backgrounds.

The reading text of *Noah and the Golden Turtle* was selected not only for its acculturation value but also for its ability to improve reading skills in the second language. According to the psycholinguistic model of reading, beginning readers must go beyond letter recognition, word recognition, and decoding to sound if they are to become fluent readers. Fluency, as defined by Kenneth Goodman, is the ability to sample text and from that sampling to predict what is to follow. (1971) The ability to predict the whole from only a part is based on the inherent redundancy in language. There are clues to meaning on many different levels of language—from phonetics to discourse. These clues reduce the alternatives from which to choose, and the reduction of alternatives leads to the "reduction of uncertainty" that is Frank Smith's definition of comprehension.*

These clues enable readers to predict. They then go on to test their predictions against information from previous samplings of the text, subsequent sampling, and their own stores of information about the topic under consideration. If the testing confirms the prediction, then the process proceeds with further sampling, and the cycle repeats itself, becoming recursive. If there is a miscue, readers pursue an alternate strategy, such as rereading or reading further, before predicting.

Second-language learners at the high-intermediate level who are literate in their own languages should not have much difficulty with the lower processing strategies of letter recognition and decoding to sound. (Their pronunciation may be poor, but they understand the concept.) They are, however, like young first-language readers: dependent on a mediated process in order to arrive at comprehension. They must go from the printed word to transla-

---

*Examples of such clue reductions include: an initial *t* can only be followed by a vowel or the letters *h, r,* or *w* (phonetic level); the plural morpheme *s* on the noun *boys* limits the subsequent verb to a plural (morphemic level); the words *the big* reduce the possible alternatives to an adjective or, more likely, a noun (syntactic level); and the word *consequently* signals that following information will be the result of preceding information.

tion in their own language. Until they are able to ———
meaning, their fluency will be hampered, for ins———
they are constrained to read word for word in ———
slow rate of speed. The strategies employe———
guage readers also can help second-lang———
need to translate.

The stories presented in this text and ———
low them are aimed at developing these highe———
(syntactic, lexical, and contextual), which in turn lead———
prediction and therefore fluency in second-language ———
ity. However, these strategies alone are insufficient if t———
matter is totally foreign because accurate testing of predic———
partially dependent on previous knowledge of the subject m———
(For example, many scientific texts written in English are almo———
entirely incomprehensible to native speakers unless they work in
the specific field.)

The choice of subject matter in this text reflects the student
population of my classroom and my desire to provide appropriate
reading material for my students—primarily Southeast Asian refu-
gees, but Latin Americans and Europeans as well. The students'
cultural backgrounds were, then, quite diverse, as is the case in
many second-language classrooms. For that reason and for the
pedagogical reasons already stated, I selected reading material
from both Asian and Western folk and religious stories.

The *Southeast Asian Research Tools*, compiled by Dr.
Charles Keyes, the *Indochinese Refugee Education Guides* of The
Center for Applied Linguistics, and my students provided me with
authentic material. It was difficult to assure familiarity with the stories on the part of all the students, so I chose stories that were
familiar in terms of locale and customs. Furthermore, it is the
nature of religious and folk stories to be fairly predictable since
many of their themes are of universal interest and concern. And,
finally, since my students were adults, I selected material that was
not too childlike.

In this text, a similar Western story is presented after each
Eastern story. This also increases the ability of students to predict
because the second story is always a version of a topic with which
they are already familiar. To further increase the usefulness of the
text, the Eastern stories have been expanded to include one from
China and one from India. (Various versions of the Indian tale are
known all throughout the Eastern world.) Their Western counterparts are from Mexico.

It is hoped, then, that the selections will both facilitate the
second-language reading process and aid in the acculturation of
the learner. Intermediate-level students have the language skills
necessary to begin using language in its integrative function, but

they must be motivated to do so. By acknowledging their cultural backgrounds and heritage in these stories and by presenting East-West counterparts, the text builds bridges between cultures. If students feel that they are not giving up their own heritage but widening it, they may be more willing to cross that bridge.

Sarah Skinner Dunn

Acknowledgments

I gratefully acknowledge Dr. Elisabeth Price of the International Institute in St. Louis for her invaluable insights and suggestions; Dr. Ann Rynearson of the International Institute, Beverly Bimes of Lindenwood Colleges, and Mary Seager of Florissant Valley Community College for their reviews of the manuscript; Emma Williams for her excellent typing; and my students at the International Institute and Webster University for their willingness and cooperation in working through the initial drafts of these stories.

Teacher's Notes

Before students begin to read the text, the teacher might briefly describe what constitutes successful reading. This is helpful for many students because they may have preconceived notions about the value of reading slowly, word by word, and looking up all unknown vocabulary.

The teacher's description may be graphically demonstrated with an illustration:

1. The teacher selects a picture, partially covers it, then asks students to identify it.
2. Students begin to find the picture more easily identifiable as more and more of the cover is removed and the whole is seen.

The reading process is somewhat the same. The meaning of one word, one sentence, or one paragraph is sometimes unclear until the entire selection has been read. For that reason, students should be encouraged to read the entire selection without looking up each unknown word. Increasing their speed of reading will also help their comprehension. If they come to the end with only a vague understanding, they should reread the selection two or three times, and each time the meaning should become clearer.

From the beginning, students should understand that it is not necessary to comprehend every word they read. Because of the inherent redundancy of language, adequate comprehension is still possible. All of the glossed words are not necessary for the student to learn, but they are needed for understanding the story, so the teacher may wish to review them before students begin reading. Glossed words that may be useful for the students' receptive vocabularies and vocabulary that may cause them problems have been selected for exercise work following each story. These exercises should help students determine the meanings of new words they encounter in their independent reading.

For those times when a dictionary is absolutely necessary, students should consult an English-English dictionary, preferably one written expressly for foreign students. Using a monolingual dictionary can be initially confusing for students. Therefore, it is helpful to provide a systematic introduction to dictionary usage. Many ESL dictionaries include such introductions.

The text itself is a collection of different types of stories: myths, legends, folk tales, religious stories, and parables. Throughout the course, the teacher may want to discuss the differences between these types.

Initial Presentation of the Story

The themes in most of the stories deal with human attitudes toward the basic concerns of life: love, fate, suffering, death, the hereafter. Before the story is read, the teacher might explore these attitudes with the class. If the teacher introduces the initial conflict or story line using carefully constructed questions, students often are able to predict the entire story before reading it.

The teacher first reads the story orally. Careful phrasing, intonation, and pronunciation will aid students' comprehension. The students themselves should not read orally because the text is not designed to improve pronunciation but reading comprehension, and oral reading on the part of students can inhibit comprehension. For homework, a second reading of each story may be assigned.

Several stories contain speed reading exercises. In these stories, the teacher should read orally up to a certain point (marked in the margin), then instruct students to read the rest of the selection as quickly as possible. When they are finished, they answer the questions in the *true/false* exercise, recording their answers in the first column. They then reread the same selection and again record their answers, this time using the second column. They should not look back at the story while doing the *true/false* exercise. These exercises demonstrate that even reading quickly allows comprehension of the essential outline of the story. The *true/false* statements are constructed with this in mind, so they are not concerned with details. When the students reread the story, the outline almost always becomes even clearer. The second column demonstrates this: a higher percentage of answers usually is correct in the second column than in the first.

Detailed Questioning

Detailed questioning should follow the initial reading of the story. These questions have not been included because the types of questions and the teacher's approach depend on the individual stories.

The general format of questions should be hierarchical in terms of difficulty: *yes/no, either/or, who/what/when/where, how/why*. With some of the simpler stories or with a more advanced class, the teacher may find it unnecessary to ask the easier kinds of questions or to analyze each sentence in detail.

The following is an example of the kind of detailed questioning the teacher might use for the second paragraph of the first story. As earlier noted, this type of questioning can be modified, depending on the needs of the class.

Did the mother take the child in her arms?

Was the child dead or alive?

Where did the mother go?

What was she asking for?

Whom did she ask to give her some medicine?

What would the medicine do?

Did the mother go to a holy man?

Was he at the first or the last house?

What was he known for?

What did he not have?

Why didn't he give her some medicine?

Vocabulary Work

A great deal of emphasis is put on vocabulary because if students hope to read successfully and efficiently in English, they must increase their vocabularies dramatically. Various types of vocabulary exercises, including vocabulary in context, synonyms, antonyms, idioms, literary expressions, the use of prepositions, two-word verbs, and word formation tables, are provided and should follow the teacher's detailed questioning. Some of these exercises may be assigned as homework and reviewed the next day in class. The idioms and literary expressions are best done in class because their meaning is often difficult for students to decipher on their own.

Because of the differences between spoken and written English, it is valuable to draw attention to those words rarely used in speech, *perish* as opposed to *die*, for example. It is also important to explain to students the theory underlying the vocabulary in context exercises. The context in which words are encountered often provides necessary clues for students' understanding of new vocabulary. Therefore, the need for a dictionary can be substantially reduced. The students must first recognize the syntactic use of the word, try to predict its meaning from their current comprehension of the story, and then check that meaning against continued reading. Frequently, the text itself contains additional clues, and the exercise is built upon these clues. For example, at times the meaning can be determined because a synonym or antonym also has been given. The use of cause and effect or of association between an object and its use can provide clues to meaning. Likewise, the use of description and example can aid comprehension. (Clarke, 1979, p. 57)

A number follows each sentence in the context and synonym exercises. This number refers students back to the paragraph or section of the story where the word appears. By seeing how the word is used both in the story and in the exercise, students should be able to determine its meaning. (A by-product of these exercises is the development of scanning skills, for students must look quickly for a specific word from a larger selection.)

Students may work through the exercises on idioms and literary expressions individually and silently in class or together as a group. Again, they should do the exercises in the context of the story. If the meaning of a word is unclear, they should refer to the expression where it appears in the story.

Two-word verbs and preposition exercises may be seen as further vocabulary work because the words they entail must be learned in the same way unfamiliar words are. Once again, students are referred to the section in the story where the two-word verb or the word-plus-preposition appears. In the writing section of each lesson, students receive additional practice in the usage of these expressions.

The word formation tables are also vocabulary-building exercises. Each word-formation table lists the word as it appears in the story and most of its derivations, though there are no specific lessons on affixes. The use of suffixes and prefixes becomes self-evident as students study the successive tables, but depending on the needs of the students, it may be advisable to introduce the most common affixes and their meanings.

The teacher should also point out differences in meaning derived from the affixes. Students should understand that many of these words are for receptive rather than productive use. The tables will help them recognize variant words that they may encounter in their independent reading. By seeing a word in different contexts and by understanding it in those different contexts, they may later be able to use it productively.

Because the negative prefix is often a source of error, it has been included, usually in its adjectival form. The teacher may point it out if it can also be used in other forms. When the negative prefix changes—for example, *dis* for the verb and *un* for the adjective—both have been included. When there is no adjective form, the teacher may point out that participles may be used as adjectives, although the meanings of past and present participles are different when they are used as adjectives.

The sole pronunciation activity in the text is presented in connection with the word formation tables because the addition of affixes frequently changes the pronunciation of a word. Therefore, when introducing a table, the teacher should pronounce each word, asking students to repeat it. Furthermore, the teacher should review the formation tables carefully before presenting them in class to assure familiarity with the usage of the words. A reinforcement exercise follows each table.

The meaning of a word, if it is unclear, can be explained briefly. Another approach is to give an unfamiliar word to each student, have him or her look for it in context, then try to arrive at an approximate meaning that may be shared with the class.

All of the words used in the vocabulary exercises, except for the idioms and literary expressions, are listed at the end of the text. After each word, a number is given, identifying the story in which the word first appears.

Structure

The text is first and foremost a reader. Therefore, the few structure exercises presented were selected primarily to clarify the reading. However, since integrated skills should not be taught in isolation, there is some emphasis on writing. One learns to write as a result of reading because by reading good material, one is exposed to good writing. Therefore, the purpose of the structure exercises is both to help clarify the reading and to improve students' writing abilities.

The structure points covered in the text are:

Selection 1	Noun clauses as objects
Selection 2	Formation of the possessive
Selection 3	Two-word verbs
Selection 4	Verbs with gerund objects or infinitive objects
Selection 6	Clauses of reason and result
Selection 7	Subjunctive after *as if* or *as though*
Selection 8	Future conditions with *were* plus infinitive
Selection 9	Reported speech

Selection 10   Past perfect
Selection 14   Verbs with only infinitive objects

If students have a firm grasp of any of the structure points outlined above, then there is no need to include that particular exercise in the lesson plan.

Reading Comprehension

Before doing the reading comprehension section, students should have heard the story once, answered questions, worked through the vocabulary exercises, and reread the story on their own. Except for "The Mustard Seed" and "The Hare-Mark on the Moon," the reading comprehension exercises take a multiple choice format. These exercises are both a testing and a teaching device. Unlike the *true/false* questions in the speed reading sections, where students answer questions from memory, students may answer these comprehension questions by consulting the text. The exercise tries to extend comprehension beyond the simpler *yes/no, wh* approach of the initial intensive questioning. The categories of comprehension it seeks to develop are:

1. Plain sense (i.e., mainly factual, exact surface meanings)
2. Implications (i.e., inference, deduced information, emotional suggestion, figurative usage, etc.)
3. Relationships of thought (i.e., between sentences/paragraphs, summarizing)
4. Projective (i.e., questions where the answers require integration of data from the text with the pupil's own knowledge and/or experience)
5. Grammatical relationships (i.e., questions that demand a response to grammatical signals, e.g., structural words, word order for emphasis, subordination, relationship of time and tense) (Munby, 1979, p. 144)

Students initially are tested on their comprehension of the story. They answer the questions individually, recording their answers both in the book and on a separate sheet of paper, which is turned in to the teacher. The teacher can then determine the extent of each student's comprehension.

Group learning follows the individual testing. The students divide into groups. (It is a good idea to place more advanced students with slower students and also to have a variety of native languages within each group to ensure that everyone speaks English.) The members of each group then compare answers with one another and try to reach a consensus. Those who have answered incorrectly learn by following the reasoning processes of the others.

Such an approach fosters rapport among students and creates a nonthreatening environment. This in turn encourages students to take risks. Risk-taking is an essential requirement for language learning. At first, the teacher may need to circulate and ask a few leading questions, but students quickly catch on to the process. After the groups have worked through the exercise, the class should correct it orally. If one group does not agree with another, each must give reasons to support its choice. Students should do as much of this work as possible, with the teacher only in the role of facilitator. An important element of that role is to direct students back to the text when there are questions. The teacher must also work through the exercise before presenting it to the class. By identifying in advance the different categories of comprehension, the teacher will be better prepared to direct students in their reasoning processes.

Dictation

Depending on how much time is allotted to the reading period in the overall class plan, dictation can be introduced at this time. Selection of suitable material is left to the teacher.

There are several different approaches to giving dictation.

1. The entire passage can be read through once at normal speed. The second reading is slower and broken up into meaningful phrases. The teacher pauses between phrases to give students time to write. The third reading is again at normal speed, during which time students check their writing.

2. In a spot dictation, except for eliminating the pauses, the teacher follows the same procedure as the one outlined above. Here, students have the passage in front of them except that certain words have been deleted and replaced by blanks. The students fill these in as the teacher reads.

3. Depending on the level of the class, a more difficult type of dictation may be given. A passage of about 100 words is read several times at normal speed by the teacher. Students then write it down from memory, using their own words when necessary. Such an approach to dictation aids students' writing abilities because they must create as well as copy.

Controlled Writing Practice

As mentioned earlier, this text places some emphasis on writing skills. It is mostly controlled writing. If the class has the ability to write independently, topics for writing are included with the topics for discussion. Most of the controlled writing exercises are self-explanatory.

Various skill practices are provided in the exercises. One is additional practice in the use of two-word verbs and prepositions. Another skill provided in several exercises throughout the text is the writing of logical questions to match short answers that are already given. Before assigning these exercises, it is helpful to review the answers in class to determine if a *wh* question is required, and if so, which one is to be used. A sentence combining exercise is also provided. This exercise, in which students recombine sentences, can provide excellent board work and discussion of the range of possible combinations. Finally, several exercises on the use of transition words are included. The teacher should explain what a transition word does and what the meanings of the transition words in the exercises are before the students attempt the exercise. Otherwise, it will be nothing more than a guessing game.* Along these lines, writing exercises in both "The Seed of Good Conversation" and "The Sun God and the Moon God" require students to put sentences in the correct order. Pointing out transition words will help them determine that order.

Topics for Discussion and Writing

Discussion and writing topics are the final activities presented in each selection unit. They attempt to explore deeper cultural and symbolic meanings in the story and therefore require a fairly high level of speaking and writing ability. The teacher must determine whether the students will profit from or be frustrated by such an activity before attempting it. If the latter is the case, I recommend omitting this section. If the teacher chooses to include it, certain topics can be developed in paragraph or composition form. If so, discussion is an important step in this development. If the teacher organizes student ideas in outline form on the board, students will be better able to organize their writing.

Independent Reading

Independent reading on the part of students is to be encouraged most of all. Offer them a wide selection of reading material from

---

*An excellent source for the teacher on the use of transition words is Ronald Mackay, "Teaching the Information-Gathering Skills," in *Reading in a Second Language*, eds. Mackay, Barkman, and Jordan (Rowley, Mass.: Newbury House, Inc., 1979), p. 88. Mackay uses the technical term *discourse marker* instead of *transition word*.

which to choose. For independent reading, books that are too easy are preferable to ones that are too difficult. Otherwise, students may become discouraged.

There are many guided readers for ESL students. Longman's series includes tales from other cultures. The Heinemann readers offer some excellent selections from English literature at an appropriate level for the ESL classroom. A visit by the teacher to the paperback section of a bookfair can yield a substantial supply of materials at nominal cost. Conrad Richter's *A Light in the Forest*, William Saroyan's *The Human Comedy*, and Pearl Buck's *The Good Earth* are a few of the possible choices for a successful and enjoyable reading experience on the part of students.

Given a willing librarian, class time spent at the neighborhood library can introduce students to the services it provides. It may also give them the incentive to use the library.

Sample Lesson Plan for Selection 7: "The Seed of Good Conversation"

At this point, an essential difference between first-language and second-language learners must be recognized. Pre-activities for the former strive to arouse students' interest. The aim is to get them mentally involved, to have them contribute their ideas, and to help them discover new ideas. For second-language learners the problem is different. They already have much they want to express but find themselves unable to do so. To attempt freewheeling discussion will only cause them frustration. Therefore, pre-activities should be carefully controlled and should give students some of the verbal tools they need to express many of the ideas they already possess. The activities described in the introduction to the Sample Lesson Plan aim at providing such a framework.

I. *Introduction (15 minutes)*

Each story should be introduced according to the following format. The teacher identifies the story type, points out its similarity to other stories, gives the main story line or conflict, and asks the class questions that lead to predicting the outcome. Any words or ideas essential to the meaning of the story also should be explained.
A. Identify the story as a legend.
   1. What do we mean by a legend? (a fictitious story, but some of the events and characters might be real)
   2. What is a myth? (a story concerned with gods, heroes, or imaginary animals; the purpose is to explain some belief or natural occurrence)

3. Have we read any myths? ("The Story of Oedipus")

B. Discuss the different types of love in the previous stories and in this one. (maternal, paternal, fraternal)

C. Introduce the conflict. (Two brothers love each other very much, but they also love the same girl.)
   1. What will one brother do?
   2. Which brother? Why?
   3. How will the younger brother feel?
   4. Do you think he will stay? What will he do?
   5. When he leaves, how will the other brother feel?
   6. Because of his guilty feelings, what will he do?
   7. What do you think the wife will do?

D. Discuss the meaning of *transformation*.

II. First Reading (30 minutes)

A. Read the story at a normal rate of speed, paying special attention to appropriate phrasing. Read as far as paragraph 11 (a natural break in the story).

B. Ask intensive questions on the first ten paragraphs. The following is an example of intensive questioning for paragraph 1.
   1. Was the mandarin's name Tan? (*yes/no*)
   2. Did he have one or two sons? (*either/or*)
   3. What were their names? (*Wh—fact*)
   4. Who confused them? (*Wh—fact*)
   5. Why did their mother confuse them? (*Wh—deductive*)
   6. Was only one boy handsome? (*yes/no*)
   7. Did they love or hate each other? (*either/or*)
   8. Who was seldom seen alone? (*Wh—fact*)
   9. Why were they always together? (*Wh—deductive*)

C. Use the same procedure for the second half of the story.

D. Assign a second reading for homework.

III.

A. Do Exercise 1 (Meaning from Context) in class.

   1. Assign sentences to the students, giving them enough time to find the word in the story and discover its meaning.
   2. Do not allow dictionaries.
   3. Have each student give the answer for his or her assigned sentence. Write the answer on the board.

B. Assign Exercises 2 and 3 (Synonyms and Antonyms) for homework, to be corrected the next day in class.

C. Do Exercise 4 (Literary Style) in class individually and silently.
   1. Encourage students to look for where the expression appears in the story.
   2. Correct the answers together orally.

D. Present the words in Exercise 5 (Word Formation Table)
  1. Have students repeat the words after you.
  2. When necessary, briefly explain meaning.
     a. Be able to give the word in a sentence to illustrate its meaning.
     b. Remind students that at this point many of the words are for receptive rather than productive use. Each time they encounter one of the words in subsequent readings, their understanding of how to use it productively will increase.
  3. Show how affixes change the meaning and syntax of the words.
     a. Have students identify noun, adjective, and adverb suffixes.
     b. Ask which noun suffix denotes a person performing an action.
     c. Ask which adjective suffix denotes ability.
     d. Draw attention to what happens to the adjective suffix -able when -ly is added.
     e. Ask what the prefix in- means. Does it always have a negative meaning? (inscribe) Are there other ways of forming the negative?
  4. Do Section B of Exercise 5 orally in class. First, ask students what part of speech is needed. Write the answers on the board.

IV. Structure (15 minutes)

  A. Explain the exercise thoroughly in class.
  B. Do the exercise orally.
  C. Assign it again as written homework.

V. Reading Comprehension (45 minutes)

  A. Mention again that this exercise is not only to test but to teach and that it is designed to increase the students' comprehension. While doing the exercise, students may refer to the story. Several choices are possible for each question, so make it clear that the best choice should be circled.
  B. Have students do the exercise silently and individually, circling their answers in the book and also writing them down on a separate piece of paper to be handed in to you.
  C. Those who finish early may go on to one of the writing exercises while waiting for the others to finish. Correct the answers as they are handed in. After collecting all the answers, divide the students into groups, assigning one person who had a high percentage of correct answers to each group.

D. Have the students work through the exercise together on a group basis. Circulate in order to help when there is a problem. If possible, do not give the correct choice yourself; rather, ask a few leading questions to focus on the level of comprehension being tested. The correct choices for the exercise are listed below, along with the category of comprehension to which each belongs (see p. xix). The suggested questions seek to develop the particular category mentioned.

1. (b) Plain sense/Implication (deduced information)
Were the brothers twins?
Would their mother have confused them if one were much older than the other?

2. (b) Plain sense/Implication (inference)
What was burned in the fire?
Is someone always poor if his or her parents die?

3. (b) Plain sense/Implication (figurative usage)
What does *vied with each other in generosity* mean?
What does *yield the hand of the girl* mean?

4. (c) Projective
Should a younger brother respect an older brother?
Why was it *his duty* to give the older brother the chopsticks?

5. (a) Implication (figurative usage)
What does *ties of blood* mean?

6. (b) Relationships of thought/Grammatical relationships
What modal means *unable*?
Why was he resting on the bank?

7. (a) Plain sense/Implication (deduced information)
What do *reproach* and *remorse* mean?
Why would Tan feel remorse?

8. (b) Plain sense
What is the meaning of *grief*?
Why was she crying?

9. (b) Plain sense/Relationships of thought
What does *marvel* mean?
What was the marvel?
When did the miracle happen?
When did the pilgrims come?

10. (b) Relationships of thought
What did the minister say was a test for a close relationship between people?
Was he able to mix the blood of the brothers?
What could he mix together?

11. (b) Plain sense
Is the betel described as a tree or a vine in the story?

12. (a) Plain sense/Grammatical relationships

If *c* is correct, what tense should the verb *begin* be in?

Do you think *presently* may have more than one meaning?

13. (c) Plain sense

What is the meaning of *a little bit?*

14. (b) Relationship of thought

What is the title of the story?

Is it a good title? Why?

VI. *Controlled Writing Practice (60 minutes)*

    A. Before assigning Exercise A, which requires the student to put the sentences in the correct order, draw attention to pronominal reference, use of articles, and transition words.

       1. *He* in the first sentence must refer to someone already mentioned. The same is true for *they* in the third sentence and *he* in the fourth.

       2. The article *a* before mandarin in the third sentence indicates that the mandarin has not been mentioned previously.

       3. *Thus* in the sixth sentence and *moreover* in the eighth are both transitional words. The former indicates that what follows is the result of something already mentioned, and the latter introduces a reinforcement of what has preceded.

    B. Assign Exercise B for homework. It would be helpful to do a summary orally with the entire class participating and a good student writing the summary on the board before students attempt to write on their own.

    C. If there is time, a passage for dictation can be given to the class. Paragraph 2 would be a good selection since students have worked with it fairly intensively. Any one of the three methods described previously (p. xx) can be used. After the students have written the passage, have them compare their writing to the story so that they recognize their mistakes right away. Circulate while they are self-correcting to help point out errors they may have missed.

VII. *Topics for Discussion and Writing (30 minutes)*

    Discuss several of the topics with the class. Write main and supporting ideas that come from the discussion on the board in outline form. If students are able to write at an independent, creative level, assign for homework a written paragraph on one of the discussion topics covered in class.

VIII. Independent Reading

Provide a list of books appropriate for the students' level. Have students check them out of the library. Require a written or oral report from each student every semester.

IX. Answer Key

At the end of the text, an answer key for the vocabulary and reading comprehension exercises is provided for the teacher or those students pursuing independent study. In a classroom situation, it may be advisable to remove the answer key from each of the student's books at the beginning of the course.

The Mustard Seed

SELECTION 1

The <u>Mustard</u> Seed

plant with yellow flowers

The following story is from Cambodia. It is one of the parables of Buddha.

1   There was once a young woman named Kassa-Godami who married the son of a rich man. She gave birth to a son, a very handsome boy whom she loved dearly. When he was old enough to walk and run on his own, he fell sick and died shortly afterwards.

The young mother took the dead child in her arms and went from house to house, asking her friends to give her a medicine that would restore life to her son. At the last house, a holy man, well known for his benevolence, said to her, "My good lady, I myself don't have such a medicine to give you, but I think I know someone who does."

"Have pity on me. Tell me to whom I must speak," said the anguished mother.

"Go find Buddha," replied the holy man, "because he can give you the medicine you need."

2   She went in search of the great Master, always carrying her small dead child in her arms. At last, having found him, she greeted him humbly and said to him, "Master, do you know of a medicine that can restore life to my child?"

"Yes," answered the Buddha, "I know how to make a medicine that can give life back to those who have lost it, but in order to make it, I need a special <u>ingredient</u>. Go, therefore, and look for a mustard seed and bring it to me. But remember one thing, my dear woman. It is essential that this mustard seed be given to you by a family who has lost neither a child, nor a husband, nor a wife, nor a parent, nor a slave."

one of the parts of a mixture

3   The woman left feeling confident and still carrying her little boy with her. The people she met would graciously say to her, "There is mustard seed here. Take as much as you want."

But when she asked, "Has there been a child, a husband, a wife, a parent, a slave who has died in this house?" they would respond, "What a strange question you ask us! The living are numerous, but the dead are even more so. Where is the house, who is the family who has not lost one of its own?"

Adapted and translated from *Contes et Legendes (Cambodge)*, Adhemard Leclere (Paris: Libraries Emile Bouillon, 1885).

And one said, "I have lost my son."

Another said, "I have lost my slave."

And others, "We have lost our parents."

4   The distressed mother could not find a single house in which there had not been a death. Slowly the light began to dawn, and she understood the thinking of the Master. She therefore returned to find the Buddha who lived in the forest.

"Have you found the mustard seed?" he asked her.

"Master," she replied, "I searched high and low, but I did not find it. Everywhere I went I was told that the living are not that numerous and the dead are innumerable."

Then the Master said to her with an air of gravity but in a tone of tenderness, "All things must pass and must change. Your intense sorrow is the sorrow of many mothers. Be then resigned and full of hope because the day will come when you will be saved. And then for you nothing more will change."

The mother slowly went away, still sad, but resigned to her misfortune.

1. **Choose the statement that best expresses the main idea of the story.**

——————   a. Suffering and death are unavoidable.

——————   b. It is impossible to get a mustard seed from a family who has not experienced death.

——————   c. All mothers experience sorrow.

2. **Synonyms:** Replace the underlined word or words with the correct synonym. The numbers in parentheses in this exercise and all that follow refer to the section in the story where the word appears. Choose from the following list:

responded, restore, benevolence, numerous, dearly, essential, anguished, gravity, distressed, special, graciously, greeted

1. The mother wanted Buddha to bring back the child's life. (1)
2. The one necessary ingredient was a mustard seed. (2)
3. The children loved the old man because of his goodwill. (1)
4. He spoke to her gently because of her sorrowful expression. (1)
5. He replied to her question. (3)
6. She was worried when she couldn't find the child. (4)
7. The soldier was cheerful in spite of the seriousness of the situation. (4)

8. She welcomed us _cordially_. (3)
9. She _welcomed_ us with a smile. (2)
10. Because of his _particular_ situation, he does not have to pay tuition. (2)
11. There are _many_ stars in the sky. (3)
12. She loved her husband _very much_. (1)

3. Antonyms: Choose the word in parentheses that completes each sentence appropriately.

1. Although very successful, he always acts (humbly/proudly).
2. The sands on the beach are (numerable/innumerable).
3. A famous person is (well known/unknown).
4. Although she had studied English for a long time, she still felt (confident/insecure) when she spoke the language.
5. A child with a (resigned/rebellious) nature is easy to care for.
6. The crime of murder is punished with (severity/tenderness).
7. When her child died, her suffering was (intense/slight).
8. In New York it is (strange/normal) for winters to be cold and summers hot.

4. Idioms and Special Expressions: Circle the letter in front of the answer that has the same meaning as the underlined expression in the context of the story.

1. Slowly, the light began to dawn.
   a. The morning was near.
   b. The light was just turned on.
   c. She began to understand.
2. The living are numerous. The dead are even more so.
   a. The dead are more numerous than the living.
   b. The living are more numerous than the dead.
   c. The number of living and dead is about even.
3. He was old enough to walk and run on his own.
   a. He was old enough to walk and run wherever he wanted.
   b. He was old enough not to need his mother.
   c. He was old enough to be able to walk and run by himself.
4. She searched high and low, but she did not find it.
   a. She looked for it on mountains and in valleys.
   b. She looked for it everywhere.
   c. She looked for it for a long time.

5. He spoke to her with an <u>air of gravity</u> but in a tone of tenderness.
   a. His face had both a gentle and a serious look.
   b. The surrounding air was heavy.
   c. His face was serious, but his voice was gentle.
6. Take <u>as much as you want.</u>
   a. Take all you want.
   b. Take as much as there is.
   c. Take much.

5A. Word Formation: When necessary, look for where the words given in the table on page 5 occur in the story. Try to determine meaning from context.

5B. Complete the following sentences with the correct form of the given word.

distress   1. Were you _____ by the news report of the accident?

question   2. Did you fill in the blanks of the _____ ?

response   3. The students in the class are very _____ .

restored   4. It is easier to _____ an old house than to build a new one.

numeral   5. The guests at the party are too _____ to count.

intensity   6. It was an _____ hot day.

confide   7. The secretary didn't read her boss' letter because it was _____ .

search   8. After having _____ everywhere, she still couldn't find her glasses.

marriage   9. What is considered the _____ age in your country?

6. Prepositions: Insert the preposition that best completes each sentence in the blank provided.

1. Do you know _____ any medicine that can restore life to my child? (2)

2. The holy man was known _____ his goodness. (1)

3. Buddha told her to look _____ a mustard seed. (2)

PARTICIPLE	NOUN	VERB	ADJECTIVE	ADVERB
confided confiding	confidence	confide	confident (3) confidential	confidently confidentially confidingly
searched searching	search searcher	search (4)		searchingly
restored restoring	restoration restorer	restore (1)	restorative	
responded responding	response responsiveness	respond (3)	responsive unresponsive	responsively
questioned questioning	question (3) questioner questionnaire	question	questionable unquestionable	questionably questioningly
distressed (4) distressing	distress	distress	distressful	distressfully distressingly
	number numeral		numerous (3) numerable innumerable (4)	
intensified intensifying	intensity	intensify	intense (4) intensive	intensely intensively
married marrying	marriage	marry (1)	marriagable	

4. She went from house to house in search_____ a special ingredient. (2)

5. She was resigned_____ her child's death. (4)

6. She asked Buddha to have pity_____ her. (1)

7. Structure: Noun clauses used as objects.

SUBJECT	VERB	DIRECT OBJECT			
		clause marker	subject	verb	complement
I	think		I	know	someone.
I	was told	that	the living	are not	that numerous.

Certain verbs can have a clause for an object. Such a clause is called a *noun clause* because the entire clause functions as a noun in the sentence. The word *that* may be included or omitted in this pattern.

7A. Listen to the statement and the words that follow. Combine them orally into one sentence.

Example: He needed a special ingredient.

He answered . . .

He answered that he needed a special ingredient.

1.	It was too late to go out.	They agreed . . .
2.	Her child's life would be restored.	She believed . . .
3.	She could find the mustard seed.	She hoped . . .
4.	She would never be happy again.	She felt . . .
5.	Buddha was teaching her a lesson.	She understood . . .
6.	Many mothers also had suffered.	She realized . . .
7.	A holy man lived in the forest.	She heard . . .
8.	He knew of someone who could help.	He said . . .
9.	Her question was strange.	They thought . . .
10.	She was carrying her child.	They noticed . . .

7B. Use the ten verbs given in the second column of Exercise 7A to make new sentences with noun clauses as objects.

Example: We understand that you just returned from vacation.

8. Reading Comprehension: Mark T (true) or F (false) in the blank after each of the following statements.

1. The boy died after he was full grown.   _____

2. At the last house the mother visited, she found   _____
    the Buddha.

3. Buddha had some special medicine with him.   _____

4. After talking to Buddha, the mother didn't bury   _____
    her son because she was sure that Buddha
    would restore his life.

5. People did not want to give the mother any   _____
    mustard seed.

6. The mother returned to Buddha when she had   _____
    found the mustard seed.

7. Buddha sent her to look for something that was   _____
    impossible to find.

8. Buddha told the mother that her sorrow would   _____
    not be permanent.

9. After she understood, the mother was happy.   _____

9A. Controlled Writing Practice: Write six sentences. In each sentence, use one of the phrases given below. Before writing the sentence, study the way the phrase is used in Exercise 6 and in the story. Then write a similar sentence.

know of, known for, look for, in search of, resigned to, have pity on

9B. Transition Words: Fill in the blanks of the sentences given below with the appropriate transition word or phrase. Choose from the list preceding each sentence.

1. rather, instead, likewise, however
    "My good lady, I myself don't have such a medicine to give you.

    _____ , I think I know someone who does."

2. yet, on the one hand, for example, therefore
    "Yes," answered the Buddha, "I know how to make a medicine that can give

    back life to those who have lost it, _____ in order to
    make it, I need a special ingredient.

3. again, nonetheless, then, yet

    "I need a special ingredient. Go, _____ , and look for a mustard seed and bring it to me."

4. consequently, at the same time, instead, rather

    "Go, therefore, and look for a mustard seed and bring it to me.

    _____ , remember one thing, my dear woman. It is essential that this mustard seed is given to you by a family who has lost neither a child nor a husband."

5. so, therefore, again, yet

    And one said, "I have lost my son." Another said, "I have lost my slave."

    _____ others, "We have lost our parents."

6. furthermore, besides, consequently, instead

    Slowly the light began to dawn, and she understood the thinking of the

    Master. _____ , she returned to find the Buddha.

7. therefore, finally, in addition, also

    "Your intense sorrow is the sorrow of many mothers. Be

    _____ resigned and full of hope because the day will come when you will be saved."

10. Topics for Discussion and Writing

      A. Why did Buddha tell the mother to look for something that was impossible to find?

      B. Why is Buddha considered a great teacher?

      C. As long as there is change, will there be suffering? Why?

      D. How does Buddha teach us to handle suffering?

The Daughter of Jairus

SELECTION 2

The Daughter of Jairus

The following story is from the New Testament. The New Testament is part of the Bible, the book upon which Christianity is based.

1   And now there came a man named Jairus, who was an official of the <u>synagogue</u>. He fell at Jesus' feet and pleaded with him to come to his house, because he had only one daughter, about twelve years old, who was dying. And the crowds were almost stifling Jesus as he went.

building used for Jewish teaching and worship

2   Now there was a woman suffering from a <u>hemorrhage</u> for twelve years, whom no one had been able to cure. She came up behind him and touched the <u>fringe</u> of his cloak and the hemorrhage stopped at that instant.

heavy bleeding

edge

Jesus said, "Who touched me?"

When they all denied that they had, Peter and his companions said, "Master, it is the crowds round you, pushing."

But Jesus said, "Somebody touched me. I felt that power had gone out from me."

Seeing herself discovered, the woman came forward trembling and, falling at his feet, explained in front of all the people why she had touched him and how she had been cured at that very moment.

"My daughter," he said "your faith has restored you to health; go in peace."

3   While he was still speaking, someone arrived from the house of the synagogue official to say, "Your daughter has died. Do not trouble the Master any further."

But Jesus had heard this, and he spoke to the man, "Do not be afraid, only have faith and she will be safe." When he came to the house, he allowed no one to go in with him except <u>Peter</u> and <u>John</u> and <u>James</u>, and the child's father and mother. They were all weeping and mourning for her, but Jesus said, "Stop crying; she is not dead, but asleep."

three of Jesus' followers

4   But they laughed at him, knowing she was dead. But taking her by the hand he called her, "Child, get up." And her <u>spirit</u> returned and she got up at once. Then he told them to give her something to

soul

Excerpt from *The Jerusalem Bible,* Copyright © 1966 by Darton, Longman & Todd, Ltd. and Doubleday & Company, Inc. Used by permission of the publisher.

eat. Her parents were astonished, but he ordered them not to tell anyone what had happened.

1. Meaning from Context: Fill in the blanks with the appropriate word. Choose from the list given below. When necessary, refer to the story to help determine meaning. The numbers in the parentheses in this exercise and in all that follow refer to the section in the story where the word appears.

fringe, denied, mourn, order, curing, cloak, crowded, companions, hemorrhage, allowed

1. He could only walk slowly because the people _____ around him. (2)

2. She had been bleeding, but after touching Jesus, her

   _____ was cured. (2)

3. James and John were _____ of Peter. (2)

4. She thanked Jesus for _____ her. (2)

5. At first everyone _____ having touched Jesus, but finally the woman admitted that it was she. (2)

6. Do people wear black in your country when they

   _____ for a relative who has died? (3)

7. The _____ of his coat almost touched the ground. (2)

8. You are not permitted to smoke in public places, but are you

   _____ to smoke in restaurants? (3)

9. Jesus was wearing a _____ , which is like a loose coat without sleeves. (2)

10. The mother did not leave many instructions, but she did

    _____ them not to open the door for anyone. (4)

2. Synonyms: Replace the underlined word or words with the correct synonym. Choose from the following list:

discovered, trouble, weeping, crowd, pleaded with, tremble, stifling, astonished, further, faith

1. She <u>begged</u> him to cure her. (1)
2. Jesus <u>found out</u> who had touched him. (2)
3. I'm sorry to <u>bother</u> you, but can you tell me the time? (3)

4. I <u>shiver</u> when I'm cold or afraid. (2)

5. The anguished mother was <u>crying</u>. (3)

6. The crowds and the <u>suffocating</u> heat made him very uncomfortable. (1)

7. We were <u>surprised</u> by her quick recovery. (4)

8. Do not say anything <u>more</u>. (3)

9. The old woman was cured because of her <u>belief</u>. (3)

10. It is impossible to <u>crush</u> any more people into the room. (2)

3. Antonyms: Choose the word in parentheses that completes each sentence appropriately.

1. In the beginning, the criminal said he was innocent, and he continues to (admit/deny) his guilt.

2. People (rejoice/mourn) when they hear good news.

3. The man was (discovered/missed) in the crowd because he was so tall.

4. The purchase of drugs without a prescription is (allowed/forbidden) in the United States.

5. Because of her (deteriorated/restored) health she was unable to lead a normal life.

6. Having been restored to (health/disease), she no longer had any pain.

4A. Word Formation: When necessary, look for where the words given in the table on page 13 occur in the story. Try to determine meaning from context.

4B. Complete the following sentences with the correct form of the given word.

tremor   1. During the earthquake, the earth_____ .

astonish   2. He looked at me in_____ .

faithful   3. The soldiers had great_____ in their leader.

mourn   4. There were many_____ at the funeral.

deny   5. The accused man_____ the charge.

laughter   6. His jokes are the source of many a_____ .

allow   7. The children were not_____ to speak in loud voices in the library.

power   8. We wanted to help her but were_____ to do so.

PARTICIPLE	NOUN	VERB	ADJECTIVE	ADVERB
allowed allowing	allowance	allow (3)	allowable	allowably
empowered empowering	power (2)	empower	powerful powerless	powerfully powerlessly
mourned mourning	mourner	mourn (3)	mournful	mournfully
denied denying	denial self-denial	deny (2)	deniable undeniable	
	faith (2) faithfulness		faithful unfaithful	faithfully
laughed laughing	laughter laugh	laugh (3)	laughable	laughably laughingly
astonished (3) astonishing	astonishment	astonish		
trembled trembling (2)	tremble tremor	tremble	tremulous	tremulously
officiated officiating	office official (3)	officiate	official	officially
suffered suffering (2)	suffering sufferer	suffer	sufferable insufferable	

suffer

9. The intense cold was _____ .

office

10. It was his _____ duty to attend all the meetings.

5. Prepositions: Insert the preposition that best completes each sentence in the blank provided.

1. They wept _____ the dying child. (3)

2. They laughed _____ him when he said the child was not dead. (4)

3. She suffered _____ an incurable disease. (2)

4. The parents mourned a long time _____ their daughter. (3)

5. A messenger arrived _____ Jairus' house. (3)

6. She touched Jesus' cloak, and _____ that moment she was cured. (2)

7. Having been cured by Jesus, the woman returned to her home

_____ peace. (2)

6. Punctuation: Special cases for the use of the apostrophe in the formation of the possessive.

A. "He fell down at Jesus' feet."

"Someone came from Jairus' house."

In words of more than one syllable that end in an *s* sound, it is permissible to form the singular possessive by adding the apostrophe without the *s*.

B. the boys' hats

the girls' faces

To form the possessive case of a plural noun ending in *s*, add the apostrophe only.

C. mother-in-law's letter

Mitchell and Symington's law firm

Mary and Jane's room

In compound (hyphenated) words, names of business firms, and words showing joint possession, only the last word is possessive in form.

6A. In the following list, the possessive relationship is expressed by means of a phrase. Change each phrase by making the noun possessive.

Example: a vacation of three weeks

  a three weeks' vacation

   1. house of Peter and John
   2. the bedroom of the girls
   3. house of my sister-in-law
   4. address of a person
   5. sailboat of John and Bob
   6. viewpoint of the editor-in-chief
   7. worth of five dollars
   8. business of Smith and Wheeler
   9. poems of William Carlos Williams
  10. testimony of the witnesses
  11. a delay of a month
  12. worth of fifteen cents
  13. events of the week
  14. coats of the ladies
  15. orders of the commander-in-chief
  16. responsibility of Tom and Charles
  17. a wait of twenty minutes
  18. rays of the sun
  19. products of Johnson and Johnson

7. Reading Comprehension: Circle the letter in front of the phrase that best completes each sentence.

   1. Jairus wanted Jesus to cure
      a. his mother who was hemorrhaging.
      b. his daughter who was dying.
      c. his wife.
   2. The daughter was
      a. exactly twelve years old.
      b. about to be twelve years old.
      c. approximately twelve years old.
   3. It was difficult for Jesus to move because
      a. the woman was touching his cloak.
      b. there were so many people around him.
      c. Jairus was at his feet.

The Daughter of Jairus   15

4. The woman had been sick for
   a. almost the entire lifetime of Jairus' daughter.
   b. most of her life.
   c. a couple of years.

5. The woman fell down in front of Jesus
   a. because the crowd pushed her.
   b. because of respect for him.
   c. because she was sick.

6. Jesus knew someone had touched him because
   a. he had seen the woman.
   b. he had felt the woman's hand.
   c. he had felt a certain power leaving him.

7. The woman was healed because
   a. she had believed in Jesus.
   b. Jesus had touched her.
   c. Jairus had pleaded with Jesus.

8. The person from the house of the synagogue official came to speak to
   a. Jairus.
   b. Jesus.
   c. Jesus' companions.

9. When Jesus raised the girl from the dead,
   a. her parents were also in the room.
   b. the crowd was watching.
   c. only he and she were in the room.

10. According to the story, the girl
   a. was only asleep.
   b. had died, but came back to life.
   c. was only sick.

8. Controlled Writing Practice

8A. Write six sentences. In each sentence use one of the phrases given below. Before writing the sentence, study the way the phrase is used in Exercise 5 and in the story. Then write a similar sentence.

weep for, laugh at, suffer from, wait for, mourn for, arrive from

8B. Combine each group of sentences into a single coherent sentence. Do not refer to the story. After writing the sentences, compare your version with the story's version.

1. There came a man. He was named Jairus. He was an official of the synagogue.
2. He pleaded with him to come to his house. He pleaded with him because he had only one daughter about twelve years old. She was dying.
3. There was a woman suffering from a hemorrhage for twelve years. No one had been able to cure her.
4. The woman saw herself discovered. She came forward. She was trembling.
5. She explained why she had touched him. She explained how she had been cured at that very moment.
6. He was still speaking. At the same time someone arrived from the house of the synagogue official.

9. Topics for Discussion and Writing

A. In what ways is this story similar to "The Mustard Seed"? In what ways is it dissimilar?
B. When Jesus cures the woman, he does not hide it from the crowd. Instead he lets the crowd know what has happened. When he cures the child, he tells the parents to tell no one. Can you think of any reasons why he would want the first miracle known and the second unknown?
C. Buddha and Christ are two of the great religious figures of the world. Who is another important religious figure? When and where did he live? Why is he important? Compare him to either Buddha or Christ.

The Golden Turtle

SELECTION 3

The Golden Turtle

Most of the stories in this text are concerned with human reactions to certain situations. These human emotions are common to all cultures. This Laotian story and the story that follows it are different. They are not about a universal human emotion, but rather an ancient human experience also common to many cultures. The experience is one of a terrible flood covering much of the earth.

1   There was once an old couple who lived on their own without any children. The man tended his fields and his garden, in which there grew rice, melons, corn, and vegetables. He also would go hunting while the old woman spun, prepared the rice, or fished with her khoeng.

a half circle made of bamboo used for fishing

2   One day while she was fishing, she found a little turtle. She set it free, went further downstream, and caught the same turtle again. She at once threw it back into the stream. The turtle let itself be caught for the third time. It must be told that this turtle was not just any turtle, but rather the Golden Turtle.

"Keep me," it said to the old woman. "I shall be useful to you."

"Very well," said the old woman, "I'll take you. You will bring a bit of life into our sad, childless home. You will belong to us and we shall be very fond of you."

3   The old man was delighted with his wife's find, and both of them spoiled their Golden Turtle. The Turtle, in return, was all kindness, gratitude, and good advice, for, apart from its gift of speech, it also had the gift of prophecy.

One day it said to the old man, "Father, in a week's time, a terrible flood will devastate the country; it will be so terrible that all the houses and all the trees will be covered with water. Therefore, you must prepare a raft and provisions."

supplies and food

The old man hurried, and, in less than a week, the raft was ready. Then it began to rain heavily. On the seventh day the river overflowed, and everything was submerged. There were only a few crafts afloat, and these were attached to trees. The water car-

covered with water/on top of the water

Adapted from "The Golden Turtle," Rene de Berval, ed., *The Kingdom of Laos* (Saigon: France Asie, 1956).

ried away tree trunks, debris of all kinds, and animals and human beings, both dead and alive.

4   The Golden Turtle said to its adopted parents, "Father and Mother, I shall dive down to look after the rope that fastens our raft to the tree; if you need me, strike the rope and I'll come to the surface."

The two old people never took a decision without first asking the advice of their adopted child and never slept at all on the raft but kept watch in turns.

One day they saw a tiger swimming toward them.

5   "Have pity on me," said the tiger, "and take me on board until the end of the flood. I shall be grateful to you."

The old people struck the rope and the turtle appeared. "A tiger is asking for protection," said the man. "Shall we take him on board?"

The turtle agreed to this idea and dived again.

Shortly afterward, a huge snake came alongside and said, "For pity's sake, take me on board until the end of the flood, and I shall be grateful to you, old woman."

The old woman called the turtle, which once again accepted the idea, so they kept the snake. Then the turtle went *place of duty* back to its observation <u>post</u>. The next time it was a man who grasped the raft saying, "I am exhausted, old man and woman. Keep me till the end and I shall be grateful to you."

The man got onto the raft, and they called the turtle.

"Since he is a human being, you cannot let him perish, Father and Mother," said the turtle, adding, "In seven days' time the waters will go down, and we shall see the earth once again."

And so they did. The three survivors said goodby to the old people and the Golden Turtle, promising to come back and see them.

went by **6**   Several months <u>elapsed</u>, and life returned again to the country. The tiger had been able to go back to the forest. Now, on one occasion when the king's daughter was going to visit the *a group of* queen of a distant country, she and her <u>entourage</u> stopped for the *personal* night in the forest. While they were asleep, the tiger came and stole *attendants* the princess' jewelry case. He kept it carefully hidden while they looked for the thief throughout the kingdom. Shortly afterward, the tiger brought the case to the old people, saying, "Here is something to repay you for your kindness to me."

7   The old folk, who did not know where the case had come from, put it right in the middle of their main room. Shortly afterward, the man they had saved came to see them and. when he saw the case, ran off to report them to the king. The old couple were arrested and thrown into prison.

8   Then the snake went to see the turtle, which told him the whole story. The snake went off to the palace, crawled into the princess' chamber and, while she was asleep, injected poison into her eyes to blind her.

For many days the princess <u>howled</u> and <u>writhed</u> in agony. The king sent for all the healers of that country and the neighboring lands, but not one of them could do anything for the princess.

screamed/ twisted and turned

9   "Let everyone come and try to cure my daughter," said the king, "and he who succeeds shall have half of my kingdom."

Then there came nobles, farmers, merchants, and fishermen, but nobody was successful in curing the princess. As the whole kingdom had tried and there was nobody left except the two poor old prisoners, the king ordered them to be brought in as well. Now, in the meantime, the snake, which had come back to see them in prison, told them what he had done and gave them a <u>root</u> that had the power to cure what he had done.

part of a plant that is underground

"In this way, you will be repaid for your generosity toward me," he told them.

So the princess was cured and the old people, by receiving half the kingdom, became king and queen in their turn.

---

1. Meaning from Context: Fill in the blanks with the appropriate word. Choose from the list given below. When necessary, refer to the story to help determine meaning. The numbers in parentheses in this exercise and all that follow refer to the section in the story where the word appears.

devastate, provisions, repaid, injected, tended, raft, perish, chamber, prophecy, submerged, survivors, palace, surface

1. He was a successful farmer because he _____ his fields every day. (1)

2. Someone who has the gift of _____ can tell what will happen in the future. (3)

3. Floods and earthquakes can _____ entire cities. (3)

4. The old man didn't drown because he had built a

_____ . (3)

5. On the boat were many _____ , so they wouldn't be hungry, thirsty, or cold. (3)

6. The waters rose so high that everything except the raft was

_____ . (3)

7. The turtle was swimming under water but would come to the

    _____ for air. (4)

8. The only people who did not _____ in the flood were those on the raft. (5)

9. The only _____ of the flood were those who were good swimmers. (5)

10. The old couple saved the snake's life and the snake

    _____ them by saving their lives. (6)

11. The medicine cannot be swallowed. It must be _____ into the veins with a needle. (8)

12. Kings and queens do not live in a small house. They live in a

    _____ . (8)

13. The princess went to her _____ because she wanted to go to sleep. (8)

2. **Synonyms:** Replace the underlined word or words with the correct synonym. Choose from the following list:

craft, fond of, spoiled, elapsed, strike, a bit of, debris, exhausted, reported, fasten, grasped, writhed, folk, howled, case

1. Everyone needs <u>some</u> happiness in life. (2)
2. Not having had children, she was <u>devoted to</u> her nieces and nephews. (2)
3. The old woman <u>pampered</u> her grandchildren. (3)
4. It took a long time to clean up all the <u>trash</u>. (3)
5. He used a rope to <u>attach</u> the boat to the tree. (4)
6. The frightened boy <u>gripped</u> his father's hand. (5)
7. He was <u>worn out</u> after the race. (5)
8. The child <u>screamed</u> when he broke his leg. (8)
9. Ten years <u>passed</u> before he returned to his native village. (6)
10. He <u>tossed</u> in pain while the doctor tried to fix the broken leg. (8)
11. When the teacher saw the boy stealing, she <u>made a complaint against</u> him to the authorities. (7)
12. The old <u>people</u> were tired. (7)
13. If you <u>hit</u> the window with a rock, it will break. (5)
14. In a flood it is useful to have any kind of <u>boat</u> that will float. (3)
15. Do you keep your jewels in a <u>box</u> or in the bank? (6)

3. Antonyms: Choose the word in parentheses that completes each sentence appropriately.

1. The ship was (afloat/submerged) in spite of the heavy rains.
2. He was loved by everyone because of his (stinginess/ generosity).
3. We were unable to see the mountain clearly because we only had a (distant/close) view.
4. We had only been given (useful/useless) information, so we didn't know what to do.
5. The doctor ordered (a poison/an antidote) for the child who had taken too many aspirins.
6. You do not need your umbrella because it is only raining (heavily/lightly).
7. The meal was so (huge/tiny) that we couldn't finish it.

4A. Word Formation: When necessary, look for where the words given in the table on page 24 occur in the story. Try to determine meaning from context.

4B. Complete the following sentences with the correct form of the given word.

1. The rocks were _____ by the flood. *submerge*

2. The boy feels very _____ toward his younger sister. *protect*

3. It only snows _____ . *occasion*

4. The city was _____ for any kind of weather. *prepare*

5. He _____ that there would be no more wars. *prophecy*

6. The _____ after the earthquake was terrible. *devastate*

7. Have they reached a _____ ? *decide*

8. Keep a _____ eye on the patient. *watch*

9. She has an _____ manner. *agree*

10. She _____ the invitation. *accept*

PARTICIPLE	NOUN	VERB	ADJECTIVE	ADVERB
submerged (3) submerging	submersion	submerge	submersible	
protected protecting	protection (5)	protect	protective	protectively
occasioned occasioning	occasion (6)	occasion	occasional	occasionally
prepared preparing	preparation preparedness	prepare (3)	preparatory	
prophesied prophesying	prophecy (3) prophet	prophesy	prophetic	prophetically
devastated devastating	devastation	devastate (3)		
decided deciding	decision (4) decision maker	decide	decisive decidable	decisively decidedly
watched watching	watch (4)	watch	watchful	watchfully
agreed agreeing	agreement disagreement	agree (5)	agreeable disagreeable	agreeably
accepted accepting	acceptance acceptability	accept (5)	acceptable unacceptable	

5. Structure: Two-Word Verbs

SUBJECT	VERB & PARTICLE
The turtle	went back.
The man	ran off.

A two-word verb consists of a verb plus an adverbial particle. The particle is part of the verb, but it changes the meaning of the verb.

5A. In the following sentences, fill in the blanks with the appropriate particle.

1. The fish he caught was too small, so he threw it

   _____ . (2)

2. The boat went_____ because there was a hole in its side. (5)

3. When will the children go_____ to school? (6)

4. The thief ran_____ with the money. (7)

5. His wife went_____ with another man. (8)

6. The judge ordered the policeman to bring_____ the thief. (9)

7. All their possessions were carried_____ in the flood. (3)

SUBJECT	VERB & PARTICLE	NOUN OBJECT	PARTICLE
They	brought in	the thief.	
They	brought	the thief	in.

When the direct object of a two-word verb is a noun, it may occur before or after the particle.

SUBJECT	VERB & PARTICLE	PRONOUN OBJECT	PARTICLE
They	brought	him	in.

When the direct object is a pronoun object, it comes between the particle and the verb.

5B. Answer the following questions with complete sentences. Use the object pronoun whenever possible.

> **Example**: Has she paid back the money?
>
> Yes, she paid **it** back last week.

1. Have the children put on their coats yet?
2. Did you turn the lights off before you left?
3. Has she called up her friend on the telephone?
4. Why did you take off your sweater?
5. What time do you wake the children up?
6. When will she get her book back?
7. Why did she go off with my sweater?
8. When will he go back to his country?
9. Did he throw back the ball?
10. Has the waiter brought the dessert in?

6. Reading Comprehension: Circle the letter in front of the phrase that best completes each sentence.

1. The old woman threw the turtle back into the stream because
   a. she didn't like turtles.
   b. she wanted it to be free.
   c. she didn't like the taste of turtle meat.
2. The turtle was able to predict
   a. the exact day of the flood.
   b. that the flood would come sometime during the week.
   c. that the flood would come sometime in the near future.
3. The raft
   a. stayed in one place.
   b. traveled over the surface of the water.
   c. was submerged by the flood.
4. The old couple
   a. watched together for problems.
   b. watched one after the other for problems.
   c. let the turtle do all the watching.
5. Of those that were saved by the old man and woman,
   a. all kept their promise to them.
   b. two kept their promise to them.
   c. none kept his promise to them.

6. The author of the story tells us
   a. that the flood lasted one week.
   b. that the flood lasted two weeks.
   c. how long it took for the waters to go up and then go down.
7. The princess was going to visit
   a. her mother, the Queen.
   b. her father, the King.
   c. another queen.
8. The old people became king and queen because
   a. they had healed the princess.
   b. while they were in prison, they listened to the turtle's advice.
   c. they had survived the flood.
9. Of the three survivors,
   a. all showed their gratitude to the old couple.
   b. two showed their gratitude to the old couple.
   c. only the snake was grateful to the old couple.

7. Controlled Writing Practice: Write seven sentences. In each sentence, use one of the two-word verbs from Exercise 5A. Before writing the sentence, study the way the two-word verb is used in Exercise 5A and in the story. Then write a similar sentence.

8. Topics for Discussion and Writing

A. Of the three survivors, the snake was the kindest to the old couple. In some cultures the snake is a symbol of evil and in others, a symbol of goodness. Which is true in your country? In what ways is it seen as good or as evil?

B. Are you familiar with any other folk tales about a terrible flood? If so, how are they similar to or different from this account?

C. A narrative is normally organized chronologically. Pick out the expressions in the story that show the progress of time. Write a paragraph in which you describe what you did and where you went from the time you left your country until you arrived in the United States. Try to use some of the time expressions from the story.

D. Thanks to the turtle's gift of prophecy, the old couple survived the flood. If you knew someone who had the gift of prophecy, would you want to know about the future or would you rather not? Discuss your reasons.

The Great Flood

The Great Flood

This story is the Western version of the flood story. Like "The Daughters of Jairus," it is from the Bible. It is, however, from the Old Testament. Judaism, as well as Christianity, is based on the books of the Old Testament.

1   As the people multiplied on the earth, their wickedness and wrongdoing multiplied even more. People were corrupt, cheating, and stealing. Everyone could see drunkedness, murder, and rioting—evil piled on evil until it was hardly safe to be alive.

So God said, "I will destroy man whom I have created. I will blot out man from the face of the earth, for I am sorry that I made him."   *destroy*

2   Yet there was one good and righteous man who tried to know the will of God. His name was Noah.   *desire*

God said to Noah, "Build yourself an ark with many rooms.   *a covered ship* Then cover it inside and out with pitch and asphalt to make it   *black sticky* watertight."   *substances*

God told Noah how to build this boat with three huge decks and a roof over the top, so it would be exactly the right size.

3   "Soon I will flood the earth to destroy every living thing," God said. "But you will ride safely in your ark along with your three sons, your wife, and your sons' wives. Now you shall bring two of every living creature into the ark: a bull and a cow, a ram and a ewe, an   *male sheep* eagle and his mate. There shall be a male and a female of every kind of bird and animal. Also, store up all kinds of food."

4   The people around Noah went on with their wild and heedless ways. Many laughed and made fun of the family of Noah. "They must be crazy," the neighbors jeered. "Look at them, building a giant boat right in the middle of a dry field!"

At last the ark was finished. God said to Noah, "Start loading the ark. In seven days rain will begin. It will rain for forty days and forty nights."

5   In seven days the waters came. The fountains of the great deep burst forth and the windows of heaven were opened. It rained and rained and rained. The waters rose, bearing up the ark.

And still it continued to rain. The waters rose so high that even the tallest mountains were covered. The thundering downpour continued for forty days and forty nights. Everything that had lived and breathed on dry land was now blotted out. Only Noah, his family, and all the creatures floating with them in the sturdy boat were left alive.

6   God did not forget Noah and his family and the animals in the ark. After a long time, the waters began to recede.

large black bird   At last the ark came to rest on a mountain. Noah opened a tiny window. Around him spread the endless lapping water.

white bird   At the end of forty days, Noah sent out a raven, but it could only fly back and forth, to and fro. Then Noah let go a dove to see if the waters had gone down anywhere. But the dove found no place

land   to light and returned.

Noah waited another seven days. In the rosy dawn he again sent the dove. In the evening the dove came back with a freshly

small, oval green or black fruit   plucked olive leaf in her mouth. So Noah knew the waters had receded at last.

7   God said to Noah, "Leave the ark, you and your family and the creatures with you. And now may you and your sons and all living things be fruitful and multiply upon the earth."

word or phrase calling for punishment   Then God said, "I will never again curse the ground because of man. Neither will I ever again destroy every living creature as I have done. While the earth remains—seedtime and harvest, cold and heat, summer and winter, day and night, shall not cease."

arch of different colors in the sky   8   So God set a rainbow in the clouds as a sign of the agreement he had made never again to destroy all life on earth.

"When I bring clouds over the earth," God promised, "and the rainbow is seen in the clouds, that will be forever the sign of my

agreement; contract   covenant."

1. Meaning from Context:

Fill in the blanks with the appropriate word. Choose from the list given below. When necessary, refer to the story to help determine meaning. The number in parentheses in this exercise and all that follow refer to the section in the story where the word appears.

mate, jeered, loaded, fruitful, harvest, watertight, deck, lapping, downpour, rosy, pitch, rioting

1. The strikers were at first peaceful, but when the government refused to listen

   to their demands, they started _____ in the streets. (1)

2. A black, sticky material used to fill cracks in ships and to make roofs

   waterproof is called _____ . (2)

3. The ship did not sink because no water could get into it. In other words, it

    was _____ . (2)

4. When you are on a ship, do you like to stand outside on the

    _____ , or do you prefer to be inside? (2)

5. The lioness is the _____ of the lion. (3)

6. The neighbors _____ Noah, but he ignored the jokes
   they made about him. (4)

7. All the animals were _____ onto the ark. (4)

8. The rainstorm was a quick but heavy _____ . (5)

9. When you look at the sky early in the morning, it often has a

    _____ color. (6)

10. When water is completely still, it makes no noise, but when it is moving

    slightly, it makes a gentle _____ noise. (6)

11. After the fall _____ , farmers are no longer so busy. (7)

12. This was a _____ year for the farmers. They had a big
    harvest. (7)

2. Synonyms: Replace the underlined word or words with the correct synonym. Choose
from the following list:

**heedless, ceased, sign, corrupt, receded, hardly, creature, multiplied,
righteous, wickedness, plucked**

1. His problems <u>increased</u> when he lost his job. (1)
2. The newspaper reported that the government official was <u>dishonest</u>. (1)
3. There was <u>barely</u> enough to eat. (1)
4. Noah and his family were the only <u>good</u> people on earth. (2)
5. Because of his <u>careless</u> manner, he did not get the job. (4)
6. All the apples had been <u>picked</u> off the trees. (6)
7. When the rain stopped, the flood water <u>went down</u>. (6)
8. The car company has <u>stopped</u> making big cars. (7)
9. The people were punished because of their <u>wrongdoing</u>. (1)
10. Two of every kind of <u>animal</u> were in the ark. (3)
11. The dove is a <u>symbol</u> of peace. (8)

3. Antonyms: Choose the word in parentheses that completes each sentence appropriately.

1. The (evil/good) man was punished for his sins.
2. I would be afraid to get into such a (sturdy/decrepit) old boat.
3. As the flood waters (receded/advanced), the mountain was slowly submerged.
4. Have you ever been up at (dawn/sunset) to see the sun rise?
5. He did such a foolish thing because he was (crazy/sane).
6. The baker sold the bread for a cheap price because it was (fresh/stale).
7. After all the guests had (remained/departed) from the party, we cleaned up.

4A. Word Formation: When necessary, look for where the words given in the table on page 33 occur in the story. Try to determine meaning from context.

4B. Complete the following sentences with the correct form of the given word.

continued   1. The _____ of the TV program will be next week.

multiply   2. We did not expect such a _____ to come to the concert.

forget   3. His _____ gets him into trouble.

fresh   4. _____ caught fish are delicious when cooked.

promised   5. She kept her _____ .

crazy   6. His _____ scares other people.

corruption   7. He lost his job because of _____ practices.

destroy   8. The storm was very _____ .

create   9. He is intelligent but not very _____ .

save   10. The drowning child was _____ by the lifeguard.

PARTICIPLE	NOUN	VERB	ADJECTIVE	ADVERB
corrupted corrupting	corruption corruptness	corrupt	corrupt (1) corruptible	
destroyed destroying	destruction destroyer	destroy (2)	destructible destructive	destructively
created (1) creating	creation creator	create	creative	creatively
saved saving	safe safety	save	safe unsafe	safely (3)
continued continuing	continuation continuity	continue (5) discontinue	continuous continual	continuously continually
multiplied multiplying	multiplication multitude	multiply (1)	multiply multitudinous	
forgotten forgetting	forgetfulness	forget (6)	forgetful forgettable	forgetfully
freshened freshening	freshness	freshen	fresh	freshly (6)
promised promising	promise	promise (8)		
	craziness		crazy (4)	crazily

5. Two-Word Verbs: In the following sentences, fill in the blanks with the appropriate particle.

1. The soldier wanted to blot _____ the memory of the war. (2)

2. The squirrel was storing_____ nuts for the winter. (3)

3. The child went_____ playing past his bedtime. (4)

4. Her courage helped to bear her_____ . (5)

5. The sun went_____ at 6 PM this evening. (6)

6. She came_____ well rested after her vacation. (6)

6. Reading Comprehension: Circle the letter in front of the phrase that best completes each sentence.

1. God decided to punish
   a. one man.
   b. all men.
   c. all men except Noah and his family.

2. In the ark there were
   a. not more than eight people.
   b. only Noah and his wife.
   c. five people.

3. It rained
   a. for seven days.
   b. for over a month.
   c. for a year.

4. God ordered Noah to load a male and female of every animal onto the ark so that
   a. they wouldn't be lonely on the long trip.
   b. all life could continue after the flood.
   c. no animals would die in the flood.

5. Noah ignored the people's laughter because
   a. he knew what was going to happen.
   b. he didn't care about them.
   c. they were evil.

6. The flood water came from
   a. windows and fountains.
   b. the ocean and the sky.
   c. the clouds.

7. Noah sent the birds out to see
   a. if they could fly.
   b. if they could find food.
   c. if they could find land.

8. The flood lasted for
    a. about eighty-seven days.
    b. forty days.
    c. eighty days.
9. According to the story, after the flood
    a. God made new life.
    b. all new life came from Noah's family and the animals on the ark.
    c. all life was destroyed.
10. God said the rainbow would be a symbol of his promise
    a. not to send anymore floods.
    b. not to destroy life on earth.
    c. not to punish man.

7. Structure: Verbs with gerund (-*ing* form) objects or infinitive objects.

SUBJECT	VERB	INFINITIVE OR GERUND OBJECT	
It	continued	to rain.	
It	continued	raining.	
The waters	began	to recede.	
The waters	began	receding.	
Noah	tried	to know	the will of God.
Noah	tried	knowing	the will of God.

Certain verbs can take both gerund objects or infinitive objects. The meaning is the same. The following is a partial list of verbs that may be followed by gerund objects or infinitive objects:

love	begin
continue	try
like	neglect
hate	prefer
start	

7A. Write two sentences for each verb in the list. The object in the first sentence should be in the gerund form, and in the second sentence it should be in the infinitive form.

Example: They attempted climbing the mountain.

They attempted to climb the mountain.

8A. Controlled Writing Practice: Write six sentences. In each sentence, use a two-word verb from Exercise 5. Before writing the sentence, study the way the two-word verb is used in Exercise 5 and in the story. Then write a similar sentence.

8B. Write logical questions for the short answers given below.

1. _____? God.

2. _____? An Ark.

3. _____? Two of every living creature.

4. _____? In seven days.

5. _____? Only Noah and his family.

6. _____? After a long time.

7. _____? To look for land.

8. _____? On a mountain.

9. _____? An olive leaf.

10. _____? The rainbow.

9. Topics for Discussion and Writing

A. Have you ever experienced a flood? Tell us what it was like.

B. The flood was sent as a punishment for men's sins. Scientific, rather than religious, reasons now explain natural disasters. Are men, however, sometimes partially responsible for natural disasters? Can you give some examples?

C. Because of this story, the rainbow is a symbol of hope and the dove bearing an olive branch is a symbol of peace in Western culture. What are some of the symbols of your culture taken from nature? Can you tell us what they symbolize and why?

The Mountain of Hope

The Mountain of Hope

1   Shortly before arriving at Lang Son, Vietnam, the traveler who goes up the Delta toward the High Country will notice at the right of the old Tonkin road a small, isolated mountain. At its summit a rock thrusts sharply upward, a tall rock that resembles the figure of a woman standing with a child in her arms. Toward evening, when the sun approaches the horizon and the statue stands out in silhouette, this resemblance becomes especially striking. This spot is called Nui Vong Phu, the "Mountain of the Woman Awaiting Her Husband." And this is her story.

separated
pushes

outlined
against the
sky

2   In former times, long ago, in a small village in these mountainous regions, there lived two orphans: a young man of twenty and his small sister, only seven years old. Because in all the world these two had only each other, they were very close.

3   One day the young man happened to consult a Chinese astrologer about the future. The astrologer said to him, "Because of the conjunction of the days and hours of your births, it seems inevitable that one day you will marry your sister. Nothing can alter the direction of your destiny."

the meeting of
two or more
stars or planets

4   This dreadful prediction appalled the young man. Day and night he was haunted by it. Finally, distracted by worry, he made a fearful decision.

shocked
deeply/returned
to mind
repeatedly

5   One day he took his little sister along with him when he went deep into the forest to cut wood. Taking advantage of a moment when she had her back turned to him, he struck her a heavy blow with his hatchet. Believing she was dead, he left her lying on the ground and fled from the spot.

6   This act, dreadful as it was, delivered him from the fear that had obsessed him. For a long time the horror of the crime he had committed pursued him, but gradually he was able to find peace of mind. He changed his name and settled down at Lang Son.

7   A number of years passed. The brother, now grown to full manhood, married the daughter of a merchant, and she bore him a son. They were a very happy family.

8   Then, one day, entering the interior courtyard of their home, the husband observed his wife in the act of drying her long black hair. She was seated in the bright sunlight under a jacaranda tree

Adapted from *Land of Seagull and Fox: Folk Tales of Vietnam*, Ruth San; Charles E. Tuttle Co., Inc., Tokyo, Japan, publisher.

with her back turned to him and did not hear him as he approached. As she slipped the comb through her sleek, damp locks, holding the hair raised high in her other hand, he saw, above the nape of her neck, a long, ugly scar.

9 At once he asked her its origin. She hesitated slightly; then, beginning to weep, she told him this story:

"I am not really the daughter of the man I call my father. I am his adopted daughter. As a small child I was an orphan, living with my older brother, the only relative I had. Fifteen years ago, for some reason I have never understood, he wounded me with an axe blow and abandoned me in the forest. I would have died there, except for the fact that some robbers saved me. A little while after that, when they were on the verge of being captured, they fled suddenly from their <u>den</u>, leaving me behind. I was discovered there by the authorities, and a little later a merchant, who had just lost his own daughter by death, took pity on me and brought me into his home to replace her. . . .

secret hiding place

"I don't know what became of my brother, and I have never been able to explain his strange act, which left me with this scar. We loved each other very much."

10 The young wife's face was bathed in tears when she had completed her story. The man mastered his own emotion with difficulty. He made her tell him the precise name of her father, and the name of her native village.

11 When it was no longer possible to doubt her true identity, he managed to keep the shocking secret to himself. But he was ashamed and revolted and felt incapable of continuing their married life. He invented a <u>pretext</u> for going away.

a false reason; an excuse

12 During the six months that his trip was supposed to last, his wife waited for him, patient and resigned. But long after that period of time had passed, she was still alone with her child.

13 Every evening she took the little boy in her arms and climbed the mountain to watch from afar for the return of the absent one. When she reached the summit, she would stand for a long time, silent, erect, her eyes fixed on the horizon.

14 Eventually she was changed into stone; and it is thus that she can still be seen, upright against the sky, motionless, eternally waiting. . . .

15 This fabled mountain with its touching story has inspired many poems. Here is one of them in approximate translation:

> Day after day, month after month, year
> after year,
> Thinking and thinking, believing, waiting
> and yet waiting. . .
> So far away, in a thousand places, my
> beloved, do you feel it—

In the sunlight, in the nighttime, through
the wind, under the rain—
This heart, eternal as gold, steadfast
as stone?

1. **Meaning from Context:** Fill in the blanks with the appropriate word from the list given below. When necessary, refer to the story to help determine meaning. The numbers in parentheses in this exercise and all that follow refer to the section in the story where the word appears.

conjunction, appalled, dreadful, summit, abandoned, consult, nape, touching, resembled, locks, inevitable, astrologer, steadfast

1. When a climber reaches the top of a mountain, he has reached

   the_____ . (1)

2. The sisters_____ each other, but their personalities were very different. (1)

3. Hair usually grows as far as the_____ of the neck. (8)

4. Although the brother tried to avoid it, his marriage to his sister was

   _____ . (3)

5. The story was_____ because of its sadness. (15)

6. _____ is a literary word for hair. (8)

7. People in the United States sometimes_____ fortunetellers when they want to know about the future. (3)

8. To kill one's sister is a_____ act. (6)

9. The brother, thinking the sister would die,_____ her. (9)

10. The discovery that his wife was his sister_____ him. (4)

11. By looking at the stars in the sky, an_____ can predict the future. (3)

12. St. Louis was built at the_____ of two rivers. (3)

13. Although her husband never returned, her love for him was

    _____ . (15)

2. **Synonyms:** Replace the underlined word or words with the correct synonym. Choose from the following list:

precise, alter, destiny, afar, dreadful, revolted, sleek, observed, erect, fled, hatchet, obsessed

1. He could not <u>change</u> his plans. (3)
2. The horse had a <u>shiny</u> coat of hair. (8)
3. She <u>ran</u> when she saw the robber. (5)
4. One cannot change one's <u>fate</u>. (3)
5. The explosion could be heard from <u>a great distance</u>. (13)
6. The news report of the murder was <u>shocking</u>. (6)
7. The smell of the dead fish <u>disgusted</u> him. (11)
8. He <u>noticed</u> the children playing in the street. (8)
9. She stands as <u>straight</u> as a statue. (13)
10. The nightmare <u>haunted</u> him the entire day. (6)
11. He cut down the tree with his <u>axe</u>. (5)
12. My watch does not keep <u>exact</u> time. (10)

3. Antonyms: Choose the word in parentheses that completes each sentence appropriately.

1. To reach the summit of the mountain, one has to climb (upward/downward).
2. Death is (inevitable/avoidable).
3. It is important to be (imprecise/precise) when giving directions.
4. To catch an airplane, one must know the (approximate/precise) time of departure.
5. The young man in the story was (capable/incapable) of abandoning his sister.
6. The (exterior/interior) of the house is heated in the winter.

4. Idioms and Special Expressions: Circle the letter in front of the answer that has the same meaning as the underlined expression.

1. The man <u>mastered his own emotion with difficulty</u>.
   a. He found it difficult to show his feelings.
   b. He found it difficult to hide his feelings.
   c. He could not master his difficulty.
2. He <u>invented a pretext</u> for going away.
   a. He told his sister the true reason.
   b. He pretended to have a reason to leave.
   c. A pretext prevented him from going away.
3. He managed <u>to keep the shocking secret to himself</u>.
   a. He told himself the secret.
   b. He didn't tell anyone else the secret.
   c. He himself was shocked by the secret.

4. She would stand for a long time, silent, erect, <u>her eyes fixed on the horizon.</u>
   a. She stared only in the direction of the horizon.
   b. Her eyes were the color of the horizon.
   c. Her eyes kept moving back and forth in search of her husband.

5A. Word Formation: When necessary, look for where the words given in the table on page 43 occur in the story. Try to determine meaning from context.

5B. Complete the following sentences with the correct form of the given word.

manage   1. Who is the _____ of this hotel?

origin   2. The student _____ lived in Europe.

explain   3. I didn't understand the teacher's _____ of the grammar rule.

destined   4. The _____ of the airplane is London.

isolate   5. The child never learned to speak because he had been kept in _____ .

distract   6. There were too many _____ .

adoption   7. Older children are not as _____ as babies.

consult   8. The doctors held a _____ to decide whether the operation was necessary.

precise   9. I would like you to come _____ at 2 PM.

observe   10. He is a good scientist because he is so _____ .

6. Prepositions: Insert the preposition that best completes each sentence in the blank provided.

1. The tall rock looks the most like a statue _____ evening. (1)

2. He was so distracted _____ worry that he was unable to sleep. (4)

3. He took his sister deep _____ the forest. (5)

4. When his sister was not looking at him, he took advantage _____ the moment and killed her with his axe. (5)

PARTICIPLE	NOUN	VERB	ADJECTIVE	ADVERB
	precision		precise (10) imprecise	precisely
managed managing	management manager	manage (11)	manageable unmanageable	
consulted consulting	consultation consultant	consult (3)		
originated originating	origin (9) originality	originate	original unoriginal	originally
explained explaining	explanation	explain (9)	explanatory explainable	
destined	destiny (3) destination	destine		
isolated (1) isolating	isolation	isolate		
distracted (4) distracting	distraction	distract	distractable	distractedly
adopted (9) adopting	adoption	adopt	adoptable adoptive	
observing observed	observation observer	observe (8)	observant unobservant	observantly observably

5. The robbers ran quickly from their hiding place because the police were on the verge _____ capturing them. (9)

6. The man took pity _____ the orphan and brought her to his home. (9)

7. He felt incapable _____ staying any longer. (11)

8. She waited a long time _____ her husband. (12)

7. Reading Comprehension: Circle the letter in front of the phrase that best completes each sentence.

1. At the top of Nui Vong Vu is
   a. a statue of a woman with her child.
   b. a rock that has been carved to look like a woman and her child.
   c. a rock that has the natural outline of a woman and her child.

2. The brother and sister had been orphans for at most
   a. seven years.
   b. their entire life.
   c. only a short while.

3. When the sun approaches the horizon,
   a. it is about to rise.
   b. it is about to set.
   c. it is high overhead.

4. The young man asked the astrologer about the future because
   a. he was worried that he might marry his sister.
   b. he was curious about his future.
   c. he wanted to change the direction of his destiny.

5. The young man attempted to kill his sister because
   a. he wanted to escape his fate.
   b. he had come to hate her because of the astrologer's prediction.
   c. his axe slipped accidentally and cut her instead of the wood.

6. After his attempted murder,
   a. he was no longer upset.
   b. he exchanged one obsession for another.
   c. he found peace of mind immediately.

7. The authorities discovered the sister
   a. because they were looking for robbers.
   b. because they were looking for the merchant's daughter.
   c. because people in the village had noticed the sister was missing.

8. The brother made up an excuse for going away because
   a. he was horrified that he had married his sister.
   b. he was afraid that she would discover who he was.
   c. he was ashamed that he had tried to kill her.
9. The main idea in this story is
   a. man's fate is inevitable.
   b. one should not be incestuous.
   c. love is eternal.

8A. Controlled Writing Practice: Write eight sentences. In each sentence, use one of the phrases given below. Before writing the sentence, study the way the phrase is used in Exercise 6 and in the story. Then write a similar sentence.

toward evening, deep into, take advantage of, on the verge of, take pity on, incapable of, distracted by, wait for

8B. In this story, there are many examples of participial phrases that modify subjects of sentences. They occur, however, at the beginning of the sentence instead of after the subject. Combine the following sentences by changing the first sentence into a non-restrictive phrase at the beginning of the new sentence.

Example: He was obssessed with his secret. He could not sleep.

Obssessed with his secret, he could not sleep.

1. He was distracted by worry. He made a fearful decision.
2. He took advantage of the moment. He struck her a heavy blow.
3. He believed she was dead. He left her lying on the ground.
4. He entered the courtyard of their home. The husband observed his wife.
5. She began to weep. She told him her story.

8C. Combine the following groups of sentences into one sentence. After completing the exercise, refer back to the story to compare your sentence with the story's sentence.

1. a. The traveler goes up the Delta toward the High Country.
    b. He will note a small isolated mountain.
    c. It is at the right of the Tonkin Road.
2. a. In all the world these two had only each other.
    b. As a result, they were very close.

3.   a. The brother was now grown to full manhood.
     b. He married the daughter of a merchant.
     c. She bore him a son.

4.   a. She was seated in the bright sunlight under a jacaranda tree.
     b. Her back was turned to him.
     c. She did not hear him as he approached.

5.   a. This act delivered him from the fear.
     b. The fear had obsessed him.

6.   a. As a small child I was an orphan.
     b. I lived with my older brother.
     c. He was the only relative I had.

7.   a. I was discovered there by the authorities.
     b. A little later a merchant took pity on me and brought me into his house to replace her.
     c. He had just lost his own daughter by death.

8.   a. I don't know what became of my brother.
     b. I have never been able to explain his strange act.
     c. It left me with this scar.

9. Topics for Discussion and Writing

A. Retell the story in your own words.

B. What conflict does the brother face at the beginning of the story? How does he solve it? Is his solution a good one? Can you think of a better solution?

C. Do some people consult astrologers in your country? If so, what questions would they ask the astrologer? To what degree would they believe in him?

a chart of the signs of the zodiac and the position of the planets

D. In the United States, some people consult their <u>horoscope</u> to find out about their future. Newspapers often have a horoscope. Look for one in the newspaper, bring it to class, and share with the class what it predicts for you.

The Story of Oedipus

The Story of Oedipus

place where questions about the future were asked of the gods

man who takes care of a group of animals

poor farmer; land often does not belong to him

cart with two wheels used in ancient times for fighting and racing

killed

troubled

a puzzling question

scared

reports/test

The Oedipus story is an ancient Greek myth. Like "The Mountain of Hope," it also is about destiny and man's effort to change it.

1   Laius, the king of Thebes, was warned by an <u>oracle</u> that there was danger to his throne and to his life if his newborn son should be allowed to grow up. Frightened by this prediction, he took the sleeping child from its crib and gave it to a <u>herdsman</u>, with orders to murder the baby. The herdsman, moved with pity, yet not daring to disobey entirely, tied up the child by the feet and left him hanging on the branch of a tree. He was found by a <u>peasant</u> who carried him to his master and mistress. The kind couple adopted him and called him Oedipus, or Swollen-foot.

2   Many years later, Laius traveled to Delphi accompanied only by one attendant. He turned into a narrow road near the city and met a young man who was driving a <u>chariot</u>. Laius ordered the young man out of his way and, because the lad was slow to obey, the attendant killed one of his horses. The stranger, filled with rage at this injustice, <u>slew</u> both Laius and his attendant. The young man was Oedipus, who unknowingly became the slayer of his own father and fulfilled the prophecy made by the oracle.

3   Shortly after this event, the citizens of Thebes were <u>molested</u> by a monster that harassed anyone nearing the city. The monster was called the Sphinx. It had the body of a lion and the upper part of a woman. It lay crouched on the top of a rock and stopped all travelers who came that way, asking them a <u>riddle</u> with the condition that those who could solve it should pass safely, but those who failed should be killed. No one had yet succeeded in solving the riddle, and all had been slain. Oedipus was not <u>daunted</u> by these alarming <u>accounts</u> and boldly advanced to the <u>trial</u>. The Sphinx asked him, "What animal is that which in the morning goes on four feet, at noon on two feet, and in the evening on three feet?"

4   Oedipus replied, "Man, who in childhood creeps on hands and knees, in manhood walks erect, and in old age walks with the aid of a staff."

5   The Sphinx was so mortified at the solving of her riddle that she cast herself down from the rocks and perished. And the grati-

Adapted from *The Age of Fable or the Beauties of Mythology,* Thomas Bulfinch (Philadelphia, Pa.: David McKay, 1898).

tude of the people of Thebes for their deliverance was so great that they made Oedipus their king, giving him in marriage their Queen, Jocasta. Oedipus, ignorant of his parentage, had already become the slayer of his father; in marrying the queen he became the husband of his mother. These horrors remained undiscovered, till <u>at length</u> Thebes <u>was afflicted with famine</u> and plague. The oracle was consulted, and the double crime of Oedipus came to light. Jocasta put an end to her life, and Oedipus went mad. He tore out his eyes and wandered away from Thebes. He was dreaded and abandoned by all except his daughters, who faithfully adhered to him, till after a long period of miserable wandering he found the <u>termination</u> of his wretched life.

finally/suffered from a time during which there is no food

end

1. **Meaning from Context:** Fill in the blanks with an appropriate word from the list given below. When necessary, refer to the story to help determine meaning. The numbers in parentheses in this exercise and all that follow refer to the section in the story where the word appears.

> **crouched, deliverance, adhered, adopted, slew, staff, molested, boldly, warned, parentage**

1. Having been _____ about the danger, Laius tried to destroy his son. (1)

2. Having been abandoned by his real father, Oedipus was
_____ by a kind couple. (1)

3. When Oedipus _____ Laius, he did not realize he was killing his father. (2)

4. The Sphinx _____ all travelers by asking them a riddle and then killing them if they could not answer it. (3)

5. The Sphinx _____ like a lion on top of the rock. (3)

6. Since Oedipus was not afraid, he walked _____ up to the Sphinx. (3)

7. The old man could still walk, but he needed to use a
_____ . (4)

8. By causing the death of the Sphinx, Oedipus was responsible for the
_____ of Thebes. (5)

9. Because his real father had abandoned him when he was a baby, Oedipus was unaware of his true _____ . (5)

10. The only people who _____ to Oedipus were his daughters. All others left him. (5)

2. Synonyms: Replace the underlined word or words with the correct synonym. Choose from the following list:

prophecy, alarming, wretched, rage, mortified, accounts, perished, daunted, harassed, termination, aid

1. In great anger, he slew the stranger. (2)
2. The prediction made by the oracle was fulfilled. (2)
3. He was not frightened by the Sphinx. (3)
4. The Sphinx troubled travelers who passed her way. (3)
5. The stories did not keep Oedipus from approaching the Sphinx. (3)
6. In spite of the frightening accounts, Oedipus was unafraid. (3)
7. The Sphinx was ashamed when he guessed the riddle. (5)
8. She died by throwing herself down from the rock. (5)
9. The rest of his life was miserable. (5)
10. After such an unhappy life, its end brought peace. (5)
11. Some old people walk with the help of a cane. (4)

3. Antonyms: Choose the word in parentheses that completes each sentence appropriately.

1. If one is not fully grown, one is still a (lad/man).
2. Not learning English will (inhibit/allow) his success in school.
3. The army, frightened by the large number of tanks and weapons, (advanced/retreated) quickly.
4. By retreating, they acted (boldly/cowardly).
5. Laius (adhered to/abandoned) his parental duties because of the oracle's warning.
6. If he (fails/succeeds) in his job, his salary will go up.
7. The daughters of Oedipus, although (ignorant/conscious) of his crime, still remained faithful to him.
8. The man's broken leg was (an aid/a hindrance) when it came to driving a car.

4. Literary Style: In the following sentences, the underlined words are used more often in writing than in speaking. Change the underlined words to what would be more typical if the sentences were spoken.

1. The Sphinx cast herself down from the rocks and perished.
2. The double crime of Oedipus came to light.
3. Jocasta put an end to her own life.
4. He found the termination of his life.

5A. Word Formation: When necessary, look for where the words given in the table on page 52 occur in the story. Try to determine meaning from context.

5B. Complete the following sentences with the correct form of the given word.

1. My promise to arrive on time is _____ upon the traffic.

   condition

2. Wolves are an _____ species.

   danger

3. Did you leave the washroom _____ a tip?

   attend

4. She should be more _____ after all the favors you have done for her.

   gratify

5. He underwent a _____ operation.

   succeed

6. The bus _____ is located downtown.

   termination

7. The pedestrian watched in _____ as the two cars crashed.

   horrible

8. His pronunciation is not good, but he _____ to the grammar rules.

   adherent

9. The people of Thebes looked upon Oedipus as their _____ .

   deliverance

10. Cancer is a terrible _____ .

    afflict

6. Structure: Clauses of reason and result.

REASON	SO (ADJECTIVE) THAT	RESULT
The Sphinx was	so mortified that	she cast herself down from the rocks.
Their gratitude was	so great that	they made Oedipus their king.
The lad was	so slow that	the attendant killed one of his horses.

Neither clause may be used alone. Sometimes <u>that</u> is omitted.

6A. Complete the following sentences with a clause of result.

Example: The pizza was so big . . .

The pizza was so big that we couldn't finish it.

PARTICIPLE	NOUN	VERB	ADJECTIVE	ADVERB
endangered endangering	danger (1) dangerousness	endanger	dangerous	dangerously
attended attending	attendant (2) attendance	attend		
succeeded (3) succeeding	success	succeed	successful unsuccessful	successfully
gratified gratifying	gratitude (5)	gratify	grateful ungrateful	gratefully
afflicted (5) afflicting	affliction	afflict	afflictive	
terminated terminating	termination (5) terminal	terminate	terminal terminable	terminally terminably
horrified horrifying	horror (5)	horrify	horrible	horribly
conditioned conditioning	condition (3)	condition	conditional unconditional	conditionally
adhered adhering	adherence adherent	adhere (5)	adherent	adherently
delivered delivering	deliverance (5) deliverer	deliver		

1. The brother was so appalled . . .

_____

2. The movie was so horrifying . . .

_____

3. His life was so miserable . . .

_____

4. The soldier was so bold . . .

_____

5. The prediction was so dreadful . . .

_____

6. The story was so touching . . .

_____

7. Her love was so steadfast . . .

_____

8. His directions were so imprecise . . .

_____

9. The two friends resembled each other so much . . .

_____

10. The prophecy was so alarming . . .

_____

RESULT (independent clause)	REASON (dependent clause)
The Sphinx cast herself down from the rocks	because she was so mortified.
The people of Thebes made Oedipus their king	since their gratitude was so great.
The attendant killed one of the lad's horses	for he was so slow.

Because is the most frequent clause marker, but *as, since,* and *for* are also used.

6B. Change the completed sentences in Exercise 6A so that the dependent clause is one of reason.

> **Example:** We couldn't finish the pizza because it was so big.

7. Reading Comprehension: Circle the letter in front of the phrase that best completes each sentence.

1. The herdsman
   a. tried to kill Oedipus.
   b. wanted to kill Oedipus.
   c. did not want to kill Oedipus.
2. Oedipus was adopted by
   a. the peasant and his wife.
   b. the herdsman.
   c. a couple for whom the peasant worked.
3. The feet of Oedipus were swollen because
   a. he had been abandoned and neglected.
   b. they had been tied tightly with a rope.
   c. they had been injured in the murder attempt.
4. The attendant killed one of
   a. the king's horses.
   b. the young man's horses.
   c. his own horses.
5. Oedipus killed his father because
   a. he wanted to fulfill the prophecy.
   b. he wanted to become king.
   c. he was furious that his horse had been killed.
6. The Sphinx could talk because
   a. it was human.
   b. it had a woman's head and face.
   c. it was a lion with magical powers.
7. Oedipus not only answered the riddle but also
   a. threw the Sphinx off its rock.
   b. killed the Sphinx.
   c. caused the Sphinx's death.
8. Jocasta killed herself because
   a. she was starving and sick.
   b. she was horrified that she had married her son.
   c. the oracle told her to.
9. Oedipus' daughters were also his half sisters because
   a. they had the same adoptive parents.
   b. they had the same mother.
   c. they had the same father.

10. Oedipus killed his father and married his mother because
    a. he hated his father and loved his mother.
    b. the oracle had told him to do it.
    c. his destiny was inevitable.

8. Controlled Writing Practice: Write logical questions for the short answers given below.

1. _____?   Laius

2. _____?   Because of the prediction

3. _____?   To the branch of a tree

4. _____?   Oedipus

5. _____?   Many years later

6. _____?   Because he was slow to obey

7. _____?   On top of a rock

8. _____?   A riddle

9. _____?   Jocasta

10. _____?   His daughters

9. Topics for Discussion and Writing

A. *Oedipus* is a Greek word that means "swollen foot." Why does Oedipus have this name?

B. Incest is a <u>taboo</u> common to all cultures. Both "Oedipus" and "The Mountain of Hope" deal with the consequences of breaking this taboo. Another taboo was also broken in each story. What was it? Can you name some taboos that all peoples share? Are there any special taboos in your society that are not taboos in this country?

act strongly forbidden by social custom

C. In both "Oedipus" and "The Mountain of Hope," man's fate is seen as inevitable. Do you think man has control over his future or is controlled by fate? What are some of your reasons for your point of view?

D. *Oedipus Complex* is a modern psychological term. It describes the feelings of a small child toward his or her parents. After reading this story, what do you think it means?

The Seed
of Good Conversation

SELECTION 7

The Seed of Good Conversation

Vietnam   Among all the legends of <u>Annam</u>, this is perhaps the best known and loved. It certainly is one of the oldest; it exists in several quite similar versions.

1   In the reign of the fourth king of the Hong Bang dynasty, there lived a mandarin by the name of Cao who had two sons, Tan and Lang. Although the two boys were not twins, they were as alike as two drops of water. Even their own mother confused them. Both boys were extremely handsome, they loved each other dearly, and one was seldom seen without the other.

2   While the brothers were still young, a fire destroyed their home, burning all the family possessions and causing the deaths of both parents. Finding themselves thus alone, without resources and friends, the brothers decided to leave together to seek work. As chance would have it, they knocked at the door of a mandarin named Lun, a very pious man who had known their father. He took the brothers into his home and developed a great affection for them, the more especially as he himself had no son, only one daughter.

3   Very soon Mandarin Lun conceived the notion of giving his daughter in marriage to one of the boys. Both the brothers were strongly attracted to the lovely girl. As for her, she could not choose between them, so alike were they in face and in spirit. Moreover, they vied with each other in generosity, each one wanting to yield to his brother the hand of the girl he was beginning to love.

4   To solve the problem, the mandarin had his daughter pre-pare a feast for the young men, hoping to discover a solution to the *situation from which there is no way out* <u>impasse</u> in the course of the banquet. First of all, at his command, the young girl brought in two bowls of steaming rice soup, with a single pair of chopsticks, and offered them to the brothers. Without a second thought, the younger brother picked up the chopsticks and presented them, as was his duty, to the elder. The mandarin then designated Tan, the elder brother, as his son-in-law.

5   Because of his deep affection for his brother and his desire to fulfill his duty toward him, Lang quickly overcame his growing love for the girl who now became his sister-in-law.

Adapted from *Land of Seagull and Fox: Folk Tales of Vietnam*, Ruth San; Charles E. Tuttle Co., Inc., Tokyo, Japan, publisher.

6   But Tan, completely <u>absorbed</u> in his new happiness, neglected the ties of blood for the first time in his life. The forsaken Lang suffered deeply in this new isolation. His suffering was the greater, in fact, because of the strength and purity of his feeling for both his brother and his sister-in-law. But, absorbed in their <u>connubial</u> bliss, the newlyweds did not notice. And so finally, unable to endure longer, Lang departed one morning from the house the three shared.

take all one's interest and time

married

7   He walked far, until finally he came to a river that he could not cross. There on the bank he rested, pondering his unhappy fate, and there death overtook him. Lang was <u>transformed</u> in death into a rock of white, chalky substance.

changed

8   When Tan noticed his brother's disappearance, he understood what had happened, and he <u>reproached</u> himself deeply for his selfishness. In <u>remorse</u>, he set out to search for Lang. After several days of walking, he, too, came to the bank of the same river. Exhausted, he sank down on the grass beside the rock and leaned against it. Soon he was also transformed, taking the shape of a tree with a very straight trunk ending in a cluster of leaves at the top, with nuts growing beneath them.

found fault with/regret for wrongdoing

9   His new wife, <u>inconsolable</u> at her husband's absence, set out in her turn. She made her way to the foot of the tree, where, completely worn out, she embraced its trunk in order not to fall. Thinking of her husband, she wept until at last she died of grief. She was transformed into a creeping vine that twined itself around the trunk of the tree.

unable to be comforted

10   Alerted by a dream, the inhabitants of the district erected a <u>pagoda</u> to the memory of the three unfortunate lovers. On its wall they inscribed these characters: "Brothers united, husband and wife devoted."

religious building

11   Later there occurred a year of exceptional <u>drought</u> when all other vegetation withered and died, and the tall tree and its tropical creeper alone retained their greenness in a sea of surrounding desolation. At the news of this marvel, <u>pilgrims</u> flocked to the pagoda from all the land.

period without rain

people who travel to a holy place

12   Finally the king himself came to visit the pagoda, and the villagers recounted to him the story of the three transformations. The king was deeply impressed and asked his counselors how he could be sure that the story was indeed true. But no one had any answers.

13   At last the Minister of Justice, a great and wise man, said to the king: "Sire, when one wishes to ascertain whether two or more persons have a close relationship, one takes some of the blood of each and mixes all the blood together in a bowl. If the mixture is closely united after <u>coagulation</u>, the answer is positive. Perhaps we could use this same test now by crushing together leaves of the creeping vine, a nut from the tree, and a fragment of the stone."

act of changing into a solid state

14   This suggestion was followed. The stone was heated and it crumbled, becoming white and soft; the vine leaves and the nut were <u>pulverized</u> and mixed with the powdered stone. Thereupon the mixture took on a beautiful deep red color, as though it were but a single substance. This was proof positive of the truth of the villagers' story.

ground into powder

15   The old minister counseled the king to have the two plants distributed widely for cultivation throughout the kingdom. This was promptly done; and, given the names "areca nuts" and "betel leaves," these products of the plants became the symbols of <u>frater-nal</u> and <u>conjugal</u> love. Presently, people began wrapping slices of the nuts together with a bit of lime paste in the leaves of the betel vine. Chewing the mixture, they found that this left a clean, invigorating taste.

brotherly married

16   The effect of this chewing can be a bit intoxicating and may seem bitter at first. But those who develop a liking for it admire the freshness, the perfume, and the marriage of sweetness with a faint bitterness. It came to be accepted that enjoying the making of the mixture and chewing it together was the best way to spark conversation; and so the serving of betel to visitors became part of Vietnamese tradition.

1. Meaning from Context: Fill in the blanks with the appropriate word. Choose from the list given below. When necessary, refer to the story to help determine meaning. The numbers in parentheses in this exercise and all that follow refer to the section in the story where the word appears.

erected, marvel, conjugal, banquet, cluster, fraternal, cultivation, faintly, twine, presented, withered

1. Steaming rice soup was served at the _____ . (4)

2. The girl _____ the rice soup to each brother. (4)

3. Leaves grow in a _____ . (8)

4. Vines often _____ themselves around a tree. (9)

5. A building is frequently _____ on the spot where a special religious event happened. (10)

6. The trees were no longer green because the leaves had all

_____ . (11)

7. A tree that stays green when everything else has withered is a

_____ . (11)

8. The _____ of the plants all over Vietnam resulted in a large crop of both betel leaves and areca nuts. (15)

9. Love between brothers is called _____ love. (15)

10. Love between husband and wife is called _____ love. (15)

11. If something is _____ bitter, it is not very bitter. (16)

2. Synonyms: Replace the underlined word or words with the correct synonym. Choose from the following list:

> forsaken, pondered, embraced, flocked, fragment, exceptional, deep, fulfill, grief, recounted to, invigorating, bliss, characters, retained, ascertain, marriage

1. The mandarin felt a <u>great</u> affection for the two boys. (5)

2. The decision to <u>perform</u> his duty made him overcome his love. (5)

3. Lang felt <u>abandoned</u> because his brother was no longer close to him. (6)

4. The <u>happiness</u> of Tan and his new wife was very great. (6)

5. While sitting on the river bank, Lang <u>thought deeply</u> about his unhappy fate. (7)

6. The wife <u>held on tightly to</u> the tree. (9)

7. Her <u>great sorrow</u> caused her death. (9)

8. The people wrote certain <u>letters</u> on the pagoda wall. (10)

9. Because there is so much rain in Vietnam, a drought is <u>out of the ordinary</u>. (11)

10. Only the tree and the vine <u>kept</u> their greenness. (11)

11. The pilgrims <u>came in large groups</u> to the pagoda. (11)

12. The villagers <u>told</u> the king the story of the three lovers. (12)

13. The king wanted to <u>find out</u> whether the story was true. (13)

14. A <u>piece</u> of the stone was crushed together with the leaf and the nut. (13)

15. The taste of the mixture was both clean and <u>exhilarating</u>. (15)

16. The <u>union</u> of both sweetness and bitterness made the mixture especially interesting. (16)

3. Antonyms: For each word in the list on the right, find the antonym in the list on the left, and write it in the blank.

transformed	1. _____	unchanged
absence	2. _____	often
depart	3. _____	negative
seldom	4. _____	shallow
deep	5. _____	arrive, remain
positive	6. _____	distracted
pious	7. _____	presence
attract	8. _____	cherish
neglect	9. _____	repel
absorbed	10. _____	unholy

4. Literary Style: Written English is often more complicated than spoken English. Match the expressions on the left with their simpler forms on the right. Write the letter in the blank.

a. set out (8)	1. _____	he died
b. as chance would have it (2)	2. _____	the midst of the drought
c. conceived the notion (3)	3. _____	immediately
d. vied with each other (3)	4. _____	competed
e. seek (2)	5. _____	go on a journey
f. yield (3)	6. _____	thought
g. without a second thought (4)	7. _____	look for
h. made her way (9)	8. _____	give
i. sea of surrounding desolation (11)	9. _____	by coincidence
j. to spark (16)	10. _____	went
k. death overtook him (7)	11. _____	to start

5A. Word Formation: When necessary, look for where the words given in the table on page 64 occur in the story. Try to determine meaning from context.

5B. Complete the following sentences with the correct form of the given word.

1. Lang was _____ by his brother.   *neglect*

2. The father was _____ to his daughter.   *devote*

3. Rice is an important _____ of Southeast   *produce*
   Asia.

4. She was unable to _____ her husband's   *endurance*
   absence.

5. To visit a graveyard at night gives me a   *creep*

   _____ feeling.

6. The king followed the advice of the wise   *counsel*

   _____ .

7. His year of illness led to a _____ in his   *transform*
   personality.

8. He could not read the _____ on the stone.   *inscribe*

9. She is an _____ good writer.   *exception*

6. Structure: Past subjunctive after *as if/as though*

INDEPENDENT CLAUSE	CLAUSE MARKER	DEPENDENT CLAUSE
The mixture took on a beautiful color	as though	it were a single substance.

After *as if/as though*, we use the past subjunctive to indicate unreality or improbability. The past subjunctive has the same form as the simple past except *were* is used instead of *was* for the third person singular of the verb *to be*. The main verb in the independent clause can either be in the present or the past.

6A. Write in the blank the appropriate form of the verb in parentheses.

Example: He spends money as if there (be) _____ no tomorrow.
            He spends money as if there **were** no tomorrow.

PARTICIPLE	NOUN	VERB	ADJECTIVE	ADVERB
consoled consoling	consolation	console	consolable inconsolable (9)	consolingly
excepted excepting	exception	except	exceptional (11) unexceptional exceptionable	exceptionally exceptionably
counseled counseling	counsel counselor (12)	counsel		
transformed (7) transforming	transformation	transform	transformable	
inscribed inscribing	inscription inscriber	inscribe (10)		
crept creeping (9)	creep creeper	creep	creepy	
neglected neglecting	neglect neglectfulness	neglect (6)	neglectful	neglectfully
endured enduring	endurance	endure (6)	endurable unendurable	enduringly
devoted (10) devoting	devotion devotee	devote	devotional	devotedly
produced producing	product (15) production	produce	productive unproductive	productively

1. The two brothers look as if they (be)_____ twins.

2. He acts as though he (not love)_____ her.

3. She acted as though it (not be)_____ difficult to leave her home.

4. He behaved as if his failure (does not)_____ bother him.

5. The student speaks English as though he (live)_____ here all his life.

6. His adoptive parents behaved as if they (be)_____ his natural parents.

7. He accepted the prediction as though it (be)_____ inevitable.

8. She recounts the story as though she (witness)_____ it herself.

9. She treats the child as though it (be)_____ her own.

10. He eats every meal as if it (be)_____ his last.

7. Reading Comprehension: Circle the letter in front of the phrase that best completes each sentence.

1. The two brothers were
   a. the same age.
   b. different ages.
   c. many years apart.
2. The boys were without possessions because
   a. their parents had died.
   b. the fire had destroyed eveything.
   c. they were orphans.
3. Each brother
   a. tried to win the girl's love for himself.
   b. tried to let the other one have the girl.
   c. decided to let the girl make up her own mind.
4. The giving of the chopsticks to Tan symbolized
   a. Lang's greater generosity.
   b. the poverty of the mandarin, since he could only afford one pair of chopsticks.
   c. Lang's respect for his older brother.
5. Lang felt extremely lonely because his brother
   a. had never before neglected their close relationship.
   b. no longer loved him.
   c. would not let him stay at the house any longer.

6. Lang remained on the river bank because
   a. he was inconsolable.
   b. the river was too difficult to cross.
   c. he wanted to think about his life.

7. Tan went to look for his brother because
   a. he felt guilty for neglecting him.
   b. he wanted to find out why Lang had left.
   c. he no longer wanted to live.

8. Tan's wife died of
   a. exhaustion.
   b. sorrow.
   c. remorse.

9. Pilgrims came to the pagoda because
   a. they had heard of the story.
   b. they wanted to see the miracle.
   c. there was nothing to eat anywhere else because of the drought.

10. The villagers' story was proven when
    a. the blood of the brothers was mixed and became one substance.
    b. only the tree and the vine remained green.
    c. the stone, leaf, and nut were mixed and became one substance.

11. The betel leaves are a product of
    a. the tree.
    b. the vine.
    c. the mixing of both the leaves of the tree and the vine together.

12. People began wrapping slices of the nuts together with a bit of lime paste in the leaves of the betel
    a. soon after the cultivation of the tree and the vine.
    b. at the same time the king gave his order for cultivation.
    c. at the present time in Vietnam.

13. The effect of chewing the betel can be
    a. very intoxicating.
    b. very bitter.
    c. slightly intoxicating.

14. One serves the betel when people come to visit
    a. to remind them of the story.
    b. because it is a good way to start a conversation.
    c. because the guests are hungry.

8A. Controlled Writing Practice: Put the following sentences in the correct order without looking at the story.

a. He took the brothers into his home and developed a great affection for them, the more especially as he himself had no son, only one daughter.

b. While the brothers were still young, a fire destroyed their home, burning all the family possessions and causing the deaths of both parents.

c. As chance would have it, they knocked at the door of a mandarin named Lun, a very pious man who had known their father.

d. Very soon Mandarin Lun conceived the notion of giving his daughter in marriage to one of the boys.

e. As for her, she could not choose between them, so alike were they in face and in spirit.

f. Finding themselves thus alone, without resources and friends, the brothers decided to set forth together to seek work.

g. Both the brothers were strongly attracted to the lovely girl.

h. Moreover, they vied with each other in generosity, each one wanting to yield to his brother the hand of the girl he was beginning to love.

8B. A summary of a story is a brief account of the story in which only the most important points are given. All details are left out. For example, a summary of paragraph 2 could be:

> The two brothers were orphaned while still young, but a mandarin adopted them.

Write a summary of paragraphs 6, 7, 8, and 9 by completing the sentences given below. Write the summary on a separate piece of paper, using paragraph form.

Lang left home because. . .

He died while resting on a river bank and. . .

Feeling guilty, Tan went to look for his brother. He also. . .

Next, Tan's wife went to look for him. Having arrived at the foot of the tree. . .

9. Topics for Conversation and Writing

A. The kind of relationship that develops between the two brothers and the girl in this story is often called a *love triangle*. Why do you think it is called that?

B. Identify the conflict in this story. What was the solution? If you wanted the solution to be a happy one, how would you rewrite it?

C. An *icebreaker* is anything that is served or done at a party to help the guests relax. Serving the betel is one kind of icebreaker. What are some other kinds of icebreakers that might be used in your country?

Pome and Peel

SELECTION 8

Pome and Peel

The following story is from Italy. It is a folk tale rather than a legend, but like "The Seed of Good Conversation," it is about love and sacrifice.

unfortunately/ away from home/magician

1   There was once a noble couple that longed to have a son, but <u>alas</u>, they had none. One day the lord was <u>abroad</u> and encountered a <u>wizard</u>. "Sir Wizard," he said, "Please tell me what I can do to have a son."

The wizard gave him an apple and said, "Have your wife eat it, and at the end of nine months she will give birth to a fine baby boy."

The husband took the apple home to his wife. "Eat this apple, and we will have a fine baby boy. A wizard told me so."

Overjoyed, the wife called her maidservant and told her to peel the apple. The maidservant did so, but kept the peeling and ate it herself.

2   A son was born to the lady, and on the same day a son was born to her maidservant. The maidservant's son was as ruddy as an apple skin; the lady's son was as white as apple pulp. The lord looked on them both as his sons and reared and schooled them together.

3   Growing up, Pome and Peel loved each other like brothers. Out walking one day, they heard about a wizard's daughter as dazzling as the sun; but no one had ever seen her, as she never went abroad or even looked out her window. Pome and Peel had a large bronze horse built with a <u>hollow belly</u>, and they hid in it with a trumpet and a violin. The horse moved on wheels the boys turned from inside, and in that manner they rolled up to the wizard's palace and began to play. The wizard looked out and, seeing that wonderful bronze horse making music all by itself, invited it inside to entertain his daughter.

stomach with an empty space inside

unmarried girl

4   The <u>maiden</u> was delighted. But the minute she was left alone with the horse, out stepped Pome and Peel, and she was

quite frightened "Don't be afraid," they said to her. "We heard how beautiful you are, and we just had to see you. If you want us to leave, we will. But if you like our music and want us to keep playing, we'll do so, then depart without letting anyone know we were here."

So they stayed on, playing and having a good time, and after a while the wizard's daughter didn't want them to leave. "Come with us," Pome told her, "and I'll marry you."

5   She accepted. They all hid in the horse's belly and off they rolled. No sooner had they gone than the wizard returned home, called his daughter, looked for her, questioned the guard at the gate: there was no sign of her anywhere. Then he realized he had been tricked, and he was furious. He went to the <u>balcony</u> and screamed three <u>curses</u> on the girl: "Let her come upon three horses—one white, one red, one black—and loving horses the way she does, let her leap on the white one, and let this horse be her undoing."

platform built on outside wall of a house/word or phrase calling for someone's punishment

"Or else: Let her come upon three pretty little dogs—one white, one red, one black—and loving little black dogs the way she does, let her pick up the black one, and let this dog be her undoing."

"Or else: On the night she goes to bed with her <u>spouse</u>, let a giant snake come through the window, and let this snake be her undoing."

husband or wife

cause of ruin

6   While the wizard was screaming those three curses from the balcony, three old <u>fairies</u> happened by on the street below and heard everything.

imaginary beings with magical powers

In the evening, weary from their long trip, the fairies stopped at an inn. As soon as they were inside, one of them remarked, "Just look at the wizard's daughter! She wouldn't be sleeping so soundly if she knew about her father's three curses!"

For there asleep on a bench in the inn were Pome, Peel, and the wizard's daughter. Peel wasn't actually asleep; perhaps he wasn't sleepy, or maybe he just considered it wiser to sleep with one eye open and thus know what was going on around him.

So he overheard one fairy say, "It's the wizard's will for her to come upon three horses—one white, one red, one black—and leap on the white one, which will be her undoing."

"But," put in the second fairy, "if some <u>far-seeing soul</u> were present, he would cut off the horse's head at once, and nothing would happen."

someone who can see into the future

The third fairy added, "Whoever breathes a word of this will turn to stone."

"Then it's the wizard's will for her to come upon three pretty little dogs," said the first fairy, "and pick up the very one that will be her undoing."

"But," commented the second fairy, "if some far-seeing soul were present, he would cut off the puppy's head at once, and nothing would happen."

"Whoever breathes a word of this," said the third fairy, "will turn to stone."

"It's finally his will, the first night she sleeps with her husband, for a giant snake to come through the window and destroy her."

"But if some far-seeing soul were present, he would cut off the snake's head, and nothing would happen," chimed in the second fairy.

"Whoever breathes a word of this will turn to stone."

So Peel found himself in possession of three terrible secrets which he could not reveal without turning to stone.

7   The next morning they set out for a post house, where Pome's father had three horses waiting for them—one white, one red, one black. The wizard's daughter immediately jumped into the saddle on the white one, but Peel promptly unsheathed his sword and cut off the horse's head.

"What are you doing? Have you lost your mind?"

"Forgive me, I am not at liberty to explain."

"Pome, this Peel has a wicked heart!" said the wizard's daughter. "I will travel no further in his company."

But Peel admitted having cut off the horse's head in a moment of madness. He begged her to forgive him, which she ended up doing.

Begin Speed Reading

8   They reached the home of Pome's parents, and three pretty little dogs ran out to meet them—one white, one red, and one black. She bent down to pick up the black one, but Peel drew his sword and cut off the dog's head.

"Away with him at once, this crazy, cruel man!" screamed the bride.

9   At that moment Pome's parents came out. They heartily welcomed their son and his bride and, learning of the dispute with Peel, they persuaded her to pardon him once more. But at dinner, *in the middle of/fun* amidst the general merriment, Peel was pensive and aloof, nor could anyone make him say what was troubling him. "Nothing's the matter, absolutely nothing," he insisted, although he left the ban- *false reason* quet early, under the pretext of being sleepy. But instead of going to his room, he entered the bridal chamber and hid under the bed.

10   The bride and bridegroom went to bed and fell asleep. Keeping watch, Peel soon heard the windowpane break, and in *took out* crawled a giant snake. Peel leaped out, bared his sword, and cut off the snake's head. At the commotion the bride awoke, saw Peel by the bed with his sword unsheathed, saw no snake (it had vanished), and screamed, "Help! Murder! Peel wants to kill us! I've

72   *Pome and Peel*

pardoned him two times already, let him be put to death this time!"

11   Peel was seized, imprisoned and three days later <u>dressed for the gallows</u>. Imagining himself now doomed in any event, he asked permission to tell Pome's wife three things before dying. She came to him in prison.

was made ready for hanging

"Do you remember," Peel asked, "when we stopped at an inn?"

"Of course I do."

"Well, while you and your husband were sleeping, three fairies came in and said the wizard had placed three curses on his daughter: to come upon three horses and leap on the white horse, which would be her undoing. But they added, should somebody quickly cut off the horse's head, nothing would happen. And whoever breathed a word of this would turn to stone."

As he said these words, poor Peel's feet and legs turned to marble.

The young woman understood. "That's enough, please!" she screamed. "Don't tell me any more!"

But he went on: "Doomed whether I speak or keep silent, I choose to speak. The three fairies also said the wizard's daughter would come upon three pretty little dogs . . ."

He related the curse regarding the little dogs and turned to stone up to his neck.

"I understand! Poor Peel, forgive me! Don't go on!" pleaded the bride.

But in a strained voice, since his throat was already marble, and stuttering, since his jaws were becoming marble, he told her about the curse with the snake. "But . . . whoever breathes a word of this . . . will turn to stone . . ." At that, he was silent, marble from head to foot.

12   "What have I done!" moaned the young wife. This faithful soul is <u>damned</u> . . . unless . . . why, of course, the only person that can save him is my father." And she took paper, pen, and ink, and wrote her father, asking his forgiveness and begging him to come to her.

punished forever

The wizard, whose child was the apple of his eye, came to her at breakneck speed. "Papa dear," she said as she kissed him, "I am asking you a favor. Look at this poor youth. After saving my life and protecting me from your three curses, he has turned to stone from head to foot."

Sighing, the wizard replied, "For the love I <u>bear</u> you, I will do this also." He drew a <u>phial of balsam</u> from his pocket, brushed Peel with it, and Peel sprang back to life as <u>sound</u> as ever.

have for small bottle with liquid from a flowering plant/healthy/ carried

Thus, instead of leading him to the gallows, they <u>bore</u> him home in triumph, amid music and singing, while the throngs around him shouted, "Long live Peel! Long live Peel!"

1. Speed Reading: Read sections 8–12 as quickly as you can. Then do the exercise, putting T (true) or F (false) in the blank next to each statement. Do not refer to the story. After completing the exercise, go back and quickly reread the same sections. Again mark T or F in the **second** column. Do not change your first answer and do not refer to the story.

1. Peel cut off his own horse's head. _____ _____

2. The wizard's daughter refused to forgive Peel for cutting off the horse's head. _____ _____

3. Pome's parents persuaded the girl to forgive Peel the second time. _____ _____

4. Peel was happy during the banquet. _____ _____

5. Peel hid under his own bed. _____ _____

6. Pome's wife wanted Peel put to death because he had killed the snake. _____ _____

7. Peel explained his strange behavior to Pome's wife because he knew he was going to die. _____ _____

8. Peel turned into stone because the wizard's daughter was angry with him. _____ _____

9. Peel stopped speaking because the wizard's daughter told him to be silent. _____ _____

10. The wizard brought Pome back to life. _____ _____

2. Meaning from Context: Fill in the blanks with the appropriate word. Choose from the list given below. When necessary, refer to the story to help determine meaning. The numbers in parentheses in this exercise and all that follow refer to the section in the story where the word first appears.

unsheathed, pulp, chamber, post house, ruddy, throngs, vanished, stuttered, breakneck, strained, doomed

1. The outside of an apple is usually a _____ color. (2)

2. The _____ of an apple is more often used in cooking than is the skin. (2)

3. Before there were cars, people went to the _____ to get horses for traveling. (7)

4. Peel kept his sword in its sheath except when he needed to cut off the horse's head. Then he _____ it. (7)

5. He went into the _____ where the newlyweds were sleeping. (9)

6. No one noticed the snake because it had _____ from the room. (10)

7. Knowing that there was no escape from death, Peel realized that he was

   _____ . (11)

8. His voice sounded _____ because his throat had turned to stone. (11)

9. Instead of speaking clearly, he _____ because his jaws no longer moved easily. (11)

10. If someone drives at _____ speed, he might have an accident and break his neck. (12)

11. The _____ filled the streets and shouted and cheered. (12)

3. Synonyms: Replace the underlined word or words with the correct synonym. Choose from the following list:

soundly, reached, crazy, sprang, dispute, pensive, bared, furious, actually, commotion, sound (adj.), reared, pardon, encountered, weary

1. He <u>raised</u> the boy as if he were his own. (2)
2. The daughter, ignorant of her father's curses, was sleeping <u>deeply</u>. (6)
3. Peel was not <u>really</u> asleep. He only appeared to be. (6)
4. Three dogs met them when they <u>arrived at</u> Pome's house. (8)
5. The girl thought Peel had gone <u>insane</u>. (8)
6. The parents were able to settle the <u>argument</u> between Peel and the girl. (9)
7. Peel was in a <u>thoughtful</u> mood at dinner. (9)
8. When he saw the snake, he <u>unsheathed</u> his sword. (10)
9. All the <u>noise</u> woke up the sleeping couple. (10)
10. The bride refused to <u>forgive</u> Peel a third time. (10)
11. Peel, transformed again by the wizard, <u>jumped</u> back to life. (12)

12. He was as <u>healthy</u> as ever. (12)
13. They were <u>exhausted</u> after their long trip. (6)
14. The girl was <u>very angry</u> with Peel. (5)
15. They had heard about the beautiful girl, but they had never <u>met</u> her. (1)

4. Antonyms: Choose the word in parentheses that completes each sentence appropriately.

1. The man was (overjoyed/depressed) when he heard the good news.
2. In the end, the child could no longer (reveal/conceal) the secret.
3. Although he is actually a friendly person, his manner seems (aloof/outgoing).
4. The soldiers' (triumph/defeat) in the battle led to the quick victory for their side.
5. Because he was (crazy/sane), the jury said he was not guilty of the crime.
6. Because he hadn't been trained for the job, his application was (accepted/rejected).
7. The girl was (delighted/appalled) when Peel cut off the dog's head.

5. Literary Style: Match the expressions on the left with their meanings on the right. Put the appropriate letter in the blank.

a. to lose one's mind	1. _____	take him away
b. not to be at liberty	2. _____	to own
c. in any event	3. _____	his favorite person
d. of course	4. _____	certainly
e. to draw a phial from his pocket	5. _____	no matter what happens
f. apple of his eye	6. _____	not to be free
g. to be in possession of	7. _____	to go crazy
h. head to foot	8. _____	to take a bottle out of his pocket
i. away with him	9. _____	entire length of the body

6A. Word Formation: When necessary, look for where the words given in the table on page 78 occur in the story. Try to determine meaning from context.

6B. Complete the following sentences with the correct form of the given word.

1. She does not have the keys in her _____ . *possess*

2. The student is _____ intelligent. *remarked*

3. After the race the runner was out of _____ . *breathe*

4. The parents were so _____ that the girl was *persuade*
no longer angry at Peel.

5. The doctor refused to _____ on the *commented*
condition of the patient.

6. A television _____ is often paid a high *entertain*
salary.

7. She is always so _____ that she gets what *insistence*
she wants.

8. It was an _____ written book. *imagination*

9. She was _____ to a banquet. *invite*

10. Sometimes it is easier to forgive than to ask for *forgive*

_____ .

7. Two-Word Verbs: Insert the particle that best completes each sentence in the blank provided.

1. Don't cut _____ your finger with that knife! (7)

2. She looked _____ to watch the parade. (3)

3. Pick _____ your clothes off the floor! (5)

4. Although the party was over, a few guests stayed

_____ . (4)

5. When she happens _____ , be sure to give her my
message. (6)

6. If one is setting _____ for a long trip, it is a good idea
to buy travelers' checks. (7)

7. The child, when he saw his mother outside, ran

_____ to greet her. (8)

PARTICIPLE	NOUN	VERB	ADJECTIVE	ADVERB
possessed possessing	possession (6) possessor	possess	possessive	possessively
entertained entertaining	entertainment entertainer	entertain (3)		entertainingly
remarked remarking	remark	remark (6)	remarkable unremarkable	remarkably
commented commenting	comment	comment (6)		
breathed breathing	breath breathlessness	breathe (6)	breathless	breathlessly
persuaded persuading	persuasion persuader	persuade (9)	persuadable persuasive	persuasively
insisted insisting	insistence insistency	insist (9)	insistent	insistently
imagined imagining (11)	imagination imaginer	imagine	imaginative imaginary	imaginatively
invited inviting	invitation inviter	invite (3)		invitingly
forgiven forgiving	forgiveness forgiver	forgive (7)	forgiveable unforgiveable	forgivingly

8. You may come _____ to play once you have finished your homework. (9)

9. Whenever there is a conversation, he always has to put

_____ his few words. (6)

8. Structure: Future conditions with "were" plus an infinitive

DEPENDENT CLAUSE (future conditional)	INDEPENDENT CLAUSE (future result)
If some far-seeing soul were present,	he would cut off the horse's head.
If some far-seeing soul were present,	he would cut off the puppy's head.
If some far-seeing soul were present,	he would cut off the snake's head.

A. In future conditions the *if* clause may contain the form *were* followed by an infinitive. The verb in the independent clause includes one of the modal auxiliaries *would, could,* or *might* plus the infinitive form of the verb without *to.*

B. Sentences with *were to* can be used for real possibilities as well as for improbabilities. Since it is a future event, it is often difficult to decide whether or not it is possible.

8C. Write sentences with *if . . . were to*, using the information given.

Example: The student might take a vacation.

(take/neglect his studies)

If he were to take a vacation, he would neglect his studies.

1. The entertainer might come.
    (come/we/be delighted)
2. The dancer might have exceptional talent.
    (have/be able to go to New York)
3. The patient might endure the pain.
    (endure/be cured quickly)
4. He might ask her to marry him.
    (ask/she/be delighted)
5. They might erect a building in this area.
    (erect/it/be dangerous because of frequent earthquakes)
6. The manager might invite us to the company's annual banquet.
    (invite/we/be sure to accept)

7. She might try to show more gratitude.
   (try/we/be glad to help her)

8. My friend might be afflicted with a terminal disease.
   (afflicted/I/be very upset)

9. The architect might adhere to the original plan.
   (adhere/the building/be too small)

10. The company might terminate the contract.
    (terminate/I/seek advice from a lawyer)

9. Reading Comprehension: Circle the letter in front of the phrase that best completes each sentence.

1. Pome and Peel
   a. were brothers.
   b. acted as if they were brothers.
   c. had the same father.

2. The horse made music because
   a. it was magical.
   b. it had a trumpet and violin inside of it.
   c. Pome and Peel were concealed inside of it and were making the music.

3. The girl wanted to depart with Pome and Peel
   a. as soon as she saw the horse.
   b. when they first appeared.
   c. after they had spent some time entertaining her.

4. The wizard knew his daughter would pick up the little black dog because
   a. the dog would be her undoing.
   b. the black dog would be the first to run out to greet her.
   c. she especially loved little black dogs.

5. The fairies in their conversation showed how someone could
   a. save the girl from the curse.
   b. keep the girl from leaping on the horse and picking up the dog.
   c. save the girl from turning into stone.

6. Peel did not explain his actions at first because he
   a. was jealous of Pome.
   b. did not want to turn to stone.
   c. hated dogs, horses, and snakes.

7. Pome's parents persuaded his bride to forgive Peel the second time because
   a. they loved him as if he were their own son.
   b. they understood his strange behavior.
   c. they didn't want him to turn to stone.

8. Peel left the feast because
    a. he was sleepy.
    b. he had to hide in the newlyweds' bedroom.
    c. he was unhappy.
9. Peel turned to stone because
    a. of the wizard's curse.
    b. the girl was angry with him.
    c. he didn't keep the fairies' secret.
10. Peel stopped speaking because
    a. the girl told him to be silent.
    b. he had been transformed into marble from head to foot.
    c. he didn't want to turn to stone.
11. The theme of this story is
    a. true friendship means being willing to give up one's life for a friend.
    b. one should never curse when one is angry.
    c. when two friends love the same girl, there is always a problem.

10A. Controlled Writing Practice: Write nine sentences. In each sentence, use one of the two-word verbs from Exercise 7. Before writing the sentence, study the way the two-word verb is used in Exercise 7 and in the story. Then write a similar sentence.

10B. Without referring to the story, combine the following groups of sentences into one sentence. Then compare your sentence to the sentence in the story.

1. a. The wife was overjoyed.
   b. The wife called her servant.
   c. She told her to peel the apple.

2. a. They went out walking one day.
   b. They heard about a wizard's daughter.
   c. She was as dazzling as the sun.

3. a. The wizard looked out.
   b. He saw that wonderful bronze horse.
   c. It was making music all by itself.
   d. He invited it inside to entertain his daughter.

4. a. So they stayed on.
   b. They played and had a good time.
   c. After awhile, the wizard's daughter didn't want them to leave.

5. a. The wizard was screaming those three curses from the balcony.
   b. At the same time three old fairies happened by on the street below.
   c. They heard everything.
6. a. In the evening the fairies were weary from their long trip.
   b. They stopped at an inn.
7. a. The next morning they set out for the post house.
   b. There Pome's father had three horses waiting for them.
8. a. They heartily welcomed their son and his bride.
   b. They learned of the dispute with Peel.
   c. They persuaded her to pardon him once more.
9. a. He recounted the curse.
   b. The curse was about the little dogs.
   c. He turned to stone.
10. a. The wizard's child was the apple of his eye.
    b. He came to her at breakneck speed.

11. Topics for Discussion and Writing

A. "The Seed of Good Conversation" is a legend and "Pome and Peel" is a fairy tale. Having read both stories, can you name some of the differences between a fairy tale and a legend? Which type of story would more frequently have a happy ending? Why?

B. The ideal friend will give up his life, and the ideal brother will give up his happiness. What other traits are important for friendship and for brotherly love?

C. Compare and contrast Peel and Lang.

Gentle Gwan Yin

SELECTION 9

Gentle Gwan Yin

1   To many Chinese, Gwan Yin, the Goddess of Mercy, is the symbol of the perfect mother. She watches over those in danger and listens to the prayers of all who suffer or are frightened. She gives children to the childless. She brings the faithful to <u>Paradise</u>, yet she refuses to enter herself as long as any living being is excluded. This is her story.

place of perfect happiness

2   In earliest times there lived an Emperor whose name was Po Chia. As he had no sons, he decided that the husband of one of his daughters would become Emperor upon his death. His favorite daughter was the youngest, who was called Miao Shan. Since Po Chia loved her best, he wanted her husband to become the next Emperor, and thus she would become Empress. But Miao Shan did not wish to marry. She told him, "I know that it is wicked to disobey my honorable father, but the glory of being an Empress is like the light of the moon reflected in a <u>stream</u>. Morning comes and it is gone. I only wish to sit quietly and pray to the gods that I may become perfect. I wish to care for the sick and help the poor."

a small river

3   Her father was furious, but she would not change her mind. Instead she begged his permission to go to the <u>convent</u> of the White Sparrow. He consented but sent word to the mistress of the convent that she was to be put in the kitchen and made to scrub floors and carry great pails of water. When these hardships did not discourage her, her father became even more enraged and sent his troops to burn the convent, but Miao Shan prayed and, in answer to her <u>supplications</u>, a deluge of rain put out the flames.

a religious home for women

prayers

4   The Emperor then brought her back to the palace and gave her the choice between life and death. She preferred death and even after hours of torture refused to change her mind. She was at last <u>strangled</u>. But the Emperor of Heaven had again heard her prayers and sent the God of the Neighborhood in the form of a tiger to rescue the princess. He carried her away into the forest and from there she descended into hell. When she opened her eyes, all was dim and still. There were no plants or flowers. No sun, moon, or stars lighted the sky. No sound was heard. No hen cackled. No dog barked. Then a young man appeared and greeted her.

to kill by squeezing the throat

Adapted from *Tales of a Chinese Grandmother*, Frances Carpenter; Charles E. Tuttle Co., Inc., Tokyo, Japan, publisher.

5   "You have come to the underworld, Miao Shan," he said. "Here, men are punished for the wrongs they have done upon the earth. The Emperor of Darkness has sent me to show you through his realm."

6   When Miao Shan saw all the poor creatures who were being punished, she began to pray for them. In answer to her prayers, the darkness was lifted and the dim underworld became a paradise of light and beauty. In fact, it was so lovely that it became entirely useless as a place of punishment and Yen-lo, the Emperor of Darkness, had to ask her to depart.

7   When she came back to earth, Miao Shan sought a quiet spot where she might think and pray and become good enough for the Heavenly Kingdom. As she wandered about, she met an old man with a huge bulging forehead. In one hand he carried a stick of gnarled wood; in the other, a peach. It was Old Long Life himself, the god who can make a man live forever. Old Long Life greeted Miao Shan and put the peach into her hands.

forehead with a large bump/twisted

"When you have eaten this peach, you will no longer feel hunger or thirst, and you will live forever," he said.

8   After Miao Shan received the gift of immortality, the God of the Neighborhood was again commanded by the Emperor of Heaven to take the form of a tiger. Upon his back he carried Miao Shan safely on a long journey to a rocky island called Pu To, which lies in the Southern Sea and where she found peace at last. For nine years the maiden prayed there. She thought only good thoughts, and at last she became perfect. Then, one day spirits and gods assembled from all the corners of the earth. From the Eastern Mountain, from the Western Mountain, from the mountains of the North and the South, and from the mountain in the center of the world they came to honor Miao Shan. The gods of the wind, the rain, and the thunder, the spirits of heaven and earth, all gathered to see her take her seat upon her golden throne, which was shaped like the lotus blossom. The Emperor of Heaven then sent her a message, telling her that she could now leave the earth and enter his kingdom. She was just about to set foot inside the shining gates of heaven when she looked back at the earth. She heard the cries of millions of poor people who were sad or in trouble, and she turned back to help them. From that time, her name was changed from Miao Shan to Gwan Yin, which means "She Who Hears Prayers."

one who lives, but without a body

9   On her rocky island in the Southern Sea there is a small temple called "The Home of Gwan Yin, who would not go away." It was built by a sailor whose life was saved by the goddess. One day this sailor was out in his boat when suddenly he found it caught in a mass of lily blossoms that covered the sea like a carpet. They grew so thickly that he could not force his way through them. Like other

flowers that grow in water

kneel and touch the ground with one's forehead

wise seamen, this sailor had on his boat a statue of Gwan Yin. He kowtowed before this saying, "Oh gentle Gwan Yin, come to my aid! Open a way through these tangled lilies. If you would go with me to my own land, so be it. Or if you would that I go to your shores, show me the way." A gentle breeze blew over the lilies. Their leaves rustled like silk as their blossoms closed tight. They sank beneath the clear water and a straight path was opened. The boatman followed its course, which led to Gwan Yin's island of Pu To. There he built a little temple and put in it the statue of Gwan Yin that had saved his life.

substance producing a sweet smell

place of worship associated with a special person or a special event

10   Gwan Yin did many wonderful things for her people. Temples were erected throughout the land to this gentle goddess. Women brought her offerings of incense and paper money. Near her statues they laid finely embroidered slippers and tiny dolls dressed like babies in the hope that she would hear their prayers for children. But her special home was always the island of Pu To, where pilgrims came by the thousands to visit her sacred shrine.

1. Meaning from Context: Fill in the blanks with the appropriate word from the list given below. When necessary, refer to the story to help determine meaning. The numbers in parentheses in this exercise and all that follow refer to the paragraph in the story where the word appears.

rustle, sacred, reflected, tortured, hell, throne, shrine, excluded, immortality, tangled, scrubbed, realm, mass, faithful, cackle

1. The _____ were allowed into Paradise, but those who sinned went to the underworld. (1)

2. The child looked into the clear water and saw his face _____ there. (2)

3. She got down on her hands and knees and _____ the dirty floor. (3)

4. They _____ her by not letting her eat or drink for several days and by keeping her all alone in a room. (4)

5. Babies cry, dogs bark, and hens _____ . (4)

6. _____ is a place where people are punished for their wrongdoing and wickedness. (4)

7. The place ruled by a king is called his _____ . (5)

8. Because she had the gift of _____ , she would never die. (8)

9. The chair of a king is called a _____ . (8)

10. Last year only a few water lilies were growing in the sea, but now there is a

    _____ of them. (9)

11. The long roots of the flowers were _____ together in the water. (9)

12. When the wind blew through the trees, we could hear the leaves

    _____ . (9)

13. Gwan Yin's _____ was the little temple built by the sailor in which he put her statue. (10)

14. The pilgrims were quiet and respectful when they visited the shrine

    because it was a _____ place. (10)

15. Anyone who was noisy was _____ from the group that was visiting the shrine. (1)

2. **Synonyms:** Replace the underlined word or words with the correct synonym. Choose from the following list:

   sought, breeze, sacred, living being, hardships, commanded, supplications, rescued, bulging, offerings, consented, the underworld, gnarled, assembled, deluge

 1. Gwan Yin wanted to help every creature reach Paradise. (1)
 2. He agreed that she could go to the convent. (3)
 3. In spite of the many difficulties, she did not consent to marriage. (3)
 4. Everything was destroyed in the flood. (3)
 5. The god answered her prayers. (3)
 6. The princess was saved by a tiger. (4)
 7. Hell was transformed into Paradise. (5)
 8. She looked for a peaceful place. (7)
 9. When we saw his swollen forehead, we wondered if it had been hit with a ball. (7)
10. His cane was made of old twisted wood. (7)
11. The god was ordered to take the shape of a tiger. (8)
12. A gentle wind rustled the leaves. (9)
13. It was a holy shrine. (10)
14. The pilgrims brought gifts to the shrine. (10)
15. The gods gathered together for the ceremony. (8)

3. Antonyms: For each word in the list on the right, find the antonym in the list on the left, and write it in the blank.

discourage	1. _____	bright
descended	2. _____	dishonorable
gentle	3. _____	included
dim	4. _____	encourage
honorable	5. _____	refused
excluded	6. _____	ascended
appeared	7. _____	placate
assemble	8. _____	disperse
enrage	9. _____	disappeared
consented	10. _____	harsh

4A. Word Formation: When necessary, look for where the words given in the table on page 89 occur in the story. Try to determine meaning from context.

4B. Complete the following sentences with the correct form of the given word.

consenting   1. She would not give her _____ to the marriage.

assemble   2. The Monday morning _____ is always at 8 o'clock.

seek   3. He _____ happiness, but he did not find it.

punish   4. What is the _____ for the crime of murder?

immortal   5. The soldier was _____ wounded in the battle.

use   6. These clothes are not very useful in this climate, but they are still _____.

perfect   7. A _____ always does everything extremely carefully.

forceful   8. They had to _____ themselves through the crowd to cross the street.

tangled   9. The string was in such a _____ that it was no longer useful.

PARTICIPLE	NOUN	VERB	ADJECTIVE	ADVERB
consented consenting	consent	consent (3)		
assembled assembling	assembly	assemble (8)		
sought seeking	seeker	seek (7)		
punished (5) punishing	punishment punisher	punish	punishable	punishingly
used using	use user usefulness uselessness	use	usable useful useless (6)	usefully uselessly
immortalized immortalizing	immortal immortality (8)	immortalize	immortal mortal	mortally
perfected perfecting	perfection perfectionist	perfect	perfect (8) imperfect	perfectly imperfectly
forced forcing	force	force (9)	forceful	forcefully
tangled (9) tangling	tangle	tangle		
hoped hoping	hope (10) hopefulness	hope	hopeful hopeless	hopefully hopelessly

hope   10. In spite of the _____ situation, she still tried
                    to be cheerful.

4C. Certain adjectives can become nouns by putting *the* in front of them. The noun
refers to a group of people.

> **Example:**   *Adjective*   *Noun*
>
>   **rich** people   the **rich**
>   **hungry** people   the **hungry**

Scan the paragraphs listed below for these types of nouns. Then
write them in the spaces provided.

paragraph 1   _____   _____

               _____   _____

paragraph 2   _____   _____

               _____   _____

               _____   _____

5. Two-Word Verbs: Insert the adverbial particle that best completes each sentence in
the blank provided.

1. He got on the airplane without looking _____. (8)

2. It is too late to turn _____. (8)

3. The mother promised the child that she would not go

   _____. (9)

4. You cannot put _____ an electric fire with water. (3)

5. Have you brought _____ the books I lent you? (4)

6. The sailboat carried them _____ across the lake. (4)

7. The two boys wandered _____ for a long time in the
   woods looking for the way out. (7)

8. The children were _____ in the fields when the storm
   started. (9)

6. Structure: Reported Speech

> The Emperor told her, "You can leave the earth and enter my
> kingdom."

Direct speech is changed to reported speech by making the direct
speech a noun clause.

The Emperor told her (that) **she could** leave the earth and enter **his** kingdom.

1. In reported speech, if the tense in the main clause is in the past, the verb in the noun clause is usually in the past or past perfect even if this is not the actual time the action occurred.

Example: Direct speech: He said, "I am tired."
Reported speech: He said that he was tired.

Direct speech: He said, "I will be tired."
Reported speech: He said that he would be tired.

Direct speech: He said, "I have been tired."
Reported speech: He said that he had been tired.

2. In reported speech, the pronouns in the noun clause are usually changed.
3. The use of "that" to introduce the noun clause is optional.
4. The noun clause is not marked by a comma.
5. The noun clause always follows the main clause.

"I do not want to be an empress," she said.

She said that she did not want to be an empress.

6A. Change the direct speech in the following sentences into reported speech.

1. Miao Shan answered, "I only wish to sit quietly and pray to the gods that I may become perfect."

_____

_____

2. "You have come to the underworld, Miao Shan," he said.

_____

_____

3. "When you have eaten this peach, you will no longer feel hunger or thirst, and you will live forever," he said.

_____

_____

4. He said, "If you would go with me to my own land, I will always be grateful."

_____

_____

5. The Emperor of Darkness said, "You will have to depart."

_____

_____

7. Reading Comprehension: Circle the letter in front of the phrase that best completes each sentence.

1. Gwan Yin
   a. is in Paradise.
   b. will not go to Paradise until everyone else is there.
   c. is waiting to become good enough for the heavenly kingdom.

2. Miao Shan did not want to be an empress because
   a. the glory of being an empress was only for a short time.
   b. she didn't want her husband to be an emperor.
   c. she didn't want to disobey her father.

3. The Emperor of Heaven came to Miao Shan's aid.
   a. one time.
   b. two times.
   c. three times.

4. The Emperor of Darkness asked Miao Shan to leave because
   a. people were suffering.
   b. she had made the underworld a place where suffering no longer existed.
   c. she was too good to be there.

5. For the Chinese, the peach is the symbol of
   a. old age.
   b. perfection.
   c. immortality.

6. Miao Shan was allowed to enter Paradise because
   a. she had received the gift of immortality.
   b. she had become perfect.
   c. she heard the cries of people in trouble.

7. Miao Shan's name was changed to Gwan Yin
   a. after rescuing the sailor.
   b. when she became immortal.
   c. when she refused to enter heaven.

8. The sailor asked Gwan Yin to take him
   a. directly back to his home.
   b. to the island of Pu To.
   c. either to his land or to hers.

9. Gwan Yin is a very special goddess because
   a. she sacrificed her happiness in order to help others.
   b. she was given the gift of immortality.
   c. she loves children.

8A. Controlled Writing Practice: Write eight sentences. In each sentence, use one of the two-word verbs from Exercise 5. Model your sentences on those used in the story and on those used in Exercise 5.

8B. Write logical questions for the answers given below.

1. _____ ?

   Miao Shan

2. _____ ?

   Because she did not want to be an empress

3. _____ ?

   In order to make her change her mind

4. _____ ?

   Into the forest

5. _____ ?

   The Emperor of Darkness

6. _____ ?

   A quiet spot

7. _____ ?

   From Old Long Life

8. _____ ?

   On the island of Pu To

9. _____ ?

   To honor Miao Shan

10. _____ ?

   When she turned back to help the poor people

11. _____ ?

   By making a straight path through the lilies

12. _____ ?

   Thousands of pilgrims

9. Topics for Discussion and Writing

A. Retell this story in your own words.

B. *Bodhisattvas* are Buddhist saints. They are described as follows: "We will become a shelter for the world, a refuge for the world, the world's place of rest, the final relief of the world, islands of the world, lights of the world, leaders of the world, the world's means of salvation." (from the *Prajñaparamita*) Given this definition, do you think Gwan Yin is a Bodhisattva? If yes, what incidents in the story of her life support your answer?

C. Describe an historical or legendary person in your country who is known for his or her self-sacrifice for the good of others.

D. Is there any shrine in your country that pilgrims visit? Who is it dedicated to? Why and when do they visit it? What do they do when they are there?

The Virgin of Guadalupe

SELECTION 10

The Virgin of Guadalupe

1   Our Lady of Guadalupe is in many ways to the Mexicans what Gwan Yin is to the Chinese. They both symbolize the perfect mother. They listen to the prayers of the needy, comfort those who suffer, heal those who are sick. This is Our Lady of Guadalupe's story.

conquerors of Mexico/ conquered

2   The legend begins in 1531, only ten years after the Spanish conquistadors had subjugated the Valley of Mexico and had introduced Christianity. An Indian who lived in the little village of Totpetlac had recently been baptized and had changed his name from Quauhtlatohua to Juan Diego. On the morning of December 9, 1531, he was walking from his village to Tlaltelolco, which was just north of Mexico City, to attend Mass and to receive religious instruction. His route passed the barren mound of Tepeyac on which nothing grew except stunted shrubs and a host of cacti. He was much depressed, as he walked along, for the Spaniards had destroyed the temple of Tonantzin, and not being quite certain which was the true faith, he was afraid that he might have displeased his native Indian goddess. Upon reaching one of the most desolate places on the side of the hill, Juan was startled and terrified to hear beautiful strains of wondrous music coming from the mountainside.

Christian ceremony by which one becomes a Christian/ Christian religious service/ small hill/ plants unable to grow very big/desert plants with thorns

3   Automatically crossing himself, for he had acquired this custom, he looked up from the trail and beheld a strange sight. He saw an arc of glorious light. In its very center, he beheld a beautiful lady, who was dressed in flowing white robes. Her lovely countenance eased his sense of fear, and she spoke in soft gentle tones that assured him of her kindliness, "Hijo mio ("my son"), come near to me."

Christian custom of making the sign of the cross with one's hand/ path/arch

one of the many names for the mother of Christ

4   He drew nearer and fell upon his knees, for it was now plain to him that she was the Virgin. She said that she wished him to go to the bishop and tell him that it was her desire that a temple be built in her honor on that very hill and that from that day forward she would be the protectress of all the Indians of Mexico.

Christian priest of high rank

5   The poor Indian pondered over what he had seen for only a brief moment. He then hurried to the Church of Santiago at

Adapted from *Of The Night Wind's Telling: Legends from the Valley of Mexico,* by E. Adams Davis. Copyright 1946 by the University of Oklahoma Press.

Tlaltelolco where he told his story to the bishop, Fray Juan de Zumarraga. The bishop listened incredulously to the Indian's story, then told him that he did not believe the tale and sent him away.

6   Sorrowfully, Juan returned to the place where the Virgin had appeared to him and found her waiting. He told her that the bishop had not believed him, and she directed him to come again on the following day. The next day was the Sabbath, and Juan again went up the hill of Tepeyac. Again the Virgin appeared to him with the order that he go a second time to take the message to the bishop.

Sunday, day of rest and worship for Christians

7   But the bishop was still unconvinced, thinking that the Holy Mother would not consider using such a poor and humble Indian for sending so important a message, and he told the man that he must bring some unmistakable token to prove that what he said was true.

evidence

8   The Indian departed, and the bishop ordered two spies to follow and watch where he went and to see with whom he talked. But, as the Indian rounded the hill, he suddenly disappeared, and, though the two spies searched the hill thoroughly, they could not find him. They therefore returned to the bishop and told him what had happened and that in their opinion Juan Diego was possessed of the devil and was guilty of witchcraft.

9   Not knowing what had happened, Juan continued to the place where he had met the Virgin. There again she appeared to him. He reported that the bishop still did not believe him and had commanded that he return with some definite token to prove beyond all doubt the truth of her commands. She reflected a moment and then said that if he would return to her on the following morning, a token would be given him that the bishop would immediately recognize.

the most powerful evil spirit/the practice of magic to make bad things happen

10   But when Juan arose the next morning, he found that his uncle, an old man called Juan Bernardino, was critically ill with the fever (called *cocolixtli* by the Aztecs) and that he must stay at home to attend him. During the day the old man steadily became worse, and the next day, which was the twelfth of December, Juan saw that his uncle was near the point of death, so he set off to the Church of Santaigo in Tlaltelolco to get a priest to come and hear the dying man's confession. Fearing that if he again met the lady, he would be delayed and his uncle would die unconfessed, he took another route around the hill of Tepeyac.

Mexican Indians

11   He had not gone far, however, when he saw her approaching, surrounded by the arc of light. Conscience-stricken for not having obeyed her orders, he fell to his knees and begged her forgiveness. But she told him not to worry, for at that moment his uncle had been healed of his sickness and was now completely well. She bade him go up the hill a little way where he would find a garden of roses and to gather and bring some of the blossoms to her, wrapped in his cloak. Her command gave a great shock to

a religious service at which a person tells his sins to a priest/sorry for having done something wrong/asked/loose clothing similar to a coat but without sleeves

Juan, for he was well acquainted with the hill and knew that it was completely barren except for the cacti and that certainly there was no garden of roses growing anywhere near. But he obeyed her command and had walked only a short distance when he came to a miraculous garden of roses just as she had described. Gathering the flowers, he wrapped them in the folds of his cloak and returned down the hill to where she was standing. She took the bundle in her arms and blessed it; then, giving it to the Indian, she told him to take the blossoms to the bishop but to be certain that no one else looked upon the roses.

Begin Speed Reading

12   Tenderly, he gathered up the flowers in his cloak and started off for the house of the bishop. But he had taken only a few steps when he heard a strange sound like that of the trickling of a little <u>brook</u> and turning around on the trail, he saw that the Virgin had disappeared but that exactly where she had stood a <u>spring</u> of clear water had burst forth from the ground. Amazed, he hurried, to the house of the bishop.

small stream

place where water comes up naturally from the ground/title of respect for a priest

13   "Again the Sainted Virgin appeared to me, my <u>Father</u>, and she bade me gather roses from the hill of Tepeyac where none have ever grown before and bring them to you wrapped in my *tilma* ("cloak"). And she said, "Tell the holy bishop that they are proof of me and that I desire that a church be built and dedicated to the Virgin of Guadalupe."

14   Then he unfolded the *tilma*, letting the roses fall to the floor, and there, miraculously painted on the cloak, was the figure of the Virgin herself. Its colors were brilliantly <u>impregnated</u> into the cloth, and it was at once clear to the bishop that no human hands had done the work.

spread completely through

15   The Virgin was of dark complexion. Her <u>features</u> were unmistakably similar to those of an Indian maiden. Her eyes were downcast, but the face was sweet and serene. She was clothed in a rose-shaded, flowing <u>gown</u> marked with gold, while over the gown she wore a long cloak of bluish velvet embroidered with golden stars. A golden cross was suspended from her throat.

the noticeable parts of a face

long dress

16   The amazed bishop, realizing that he had witnessed a miracle, fell to his knees in <u>veneration</u> of the Virgin, then arose and placed the sacred cloak in the <u>oratory</u> of the church. The Indian returned home and found his uncle well again. He had been cured exactly at the moment when the Virgin had spoken her words of encouragement.

treating with great honor/ section of the church used for praying

17   The following day the bishop, accompanied by a large <u>train</u> of churchmen, visited the house of Juan and spoke to the man who had been miraculously healed. Guided by the Indian, they visited the spot where the Virgin had spoken to him and where the spring of clear water now flowed, and there the bishop and the priests prayed to the Virgin and promised her that a church would be built on the hill of Tepeyac, just as she had ordered.

group of people attending a person of high rank

18   The news of the miracle spread rapidly throughout the whole of Mexico. Great crowds of people came to the palace of the bishop to see the painting of the Holy Virgin on the *tilma* of the poor Indian. So great were the crowds that the bishop had to take the cloak to the great cathedral in the City of Mexico in order that all might see it; and so many converts came to the little hill of Tepeyac that there were not enough priests to baptize them.

people who have been persuaded to accept a particular religion

19   The bishop took charge of the situation, and within three months a shrine had been constructed over the exact spot indicated by the Virgin. The *tilma* with its holy image was then placed over the altar and the people continued to visit the shrine. Spaniards called it Our Lady of Guadalupe, in honor of the Geronimite Convent of Guadalupe in Spain, but to the Indian it was *La Virgen India de Tepeyac* (the Indian Virgin of Tepeyac). Juan Diego became an attendant of the shrine and remained in the home of the Virgin until his death in 1548.

20   The Shrine of the Virgin of Guadalupe has become a national shrine and, more important, its Virgin is the patron saint of the Mexican Indian. During the centuries since the founding of the little chapel on its summit, it has been the place toward which the Indians have turned for spiritual consolation. To their shrine they come during all the seasons of the year, from all parts of the country.

holy person who gives special protection to a certain group

1. Speed Reading: Read sections 12–20 as quickly as you can. Then do the exercise, putting T (true) or F (false) in the **first** blank next to each statement. Do not refer to the story. After completing the exercise, go back and quickly reread the same sections. Again mark T or F in the **second** column. Do not change your first answer and do not refer to the story.

1. Juan Diego left the roses with the Virgin.   _____   _____

2. A spring appeared where the Virgin had been standing.   _____   _____

3. When Juan opened his cloak, the bishop saw a picture of the roses on it.   _____   _____

4. The Virgin looked like an Indian.   _____   _____

5. The bishop was cured of his illness when he looked at the picture.   _____   _____

6. A church was built on the spot where the Virgin had spoken to Juan Diego. _____ _____

7. The cloak with its image was always kept in the cathedral in Mexico City. _____ _____

8. Many people came to Tepeyac in order to be baptized. _____ _____

9. The Indians gave the Virgin the name "Our Lady of Guadalupe." _____ _____

10. The Virgin of Guadalupe is the patron saint of the Indians in Mexico. _____ _____

2. Meaning from Context: Fill in the blanks with the appropriate word from the list given below. When necessary, refer to the story to help determine meaning. The numbers in parentheses in this exercise and all that follow refer to the section in the story where the word appears.

host, incredulous, subjugated, delayed, critically, beheld, route, shock, complexion, assured, protectress, barren, stunted, spies

1. The Mexican Indians fought the Spaniards, but they were finally

   _____ . (2)

2. When Juan Diego walked to Mexico City, he always took the same

   _____ . (2)

3. The hill was_____ because there was little rainfall, and therefore nothing would grow. (2)

4. The trees and bushes were_____ because they could not grow without rain. (2)

5. The plural of cactus is cacti, and when a group of cacti grow together, the

   group is called a_____ of cacti. (2)

6. At first he didn't see anything, but when he looked more carefully, he

   _____ a beautiful sight. (3)

7. In the beginning he was afraid, but when he heard her kind voice, he was

   _____ that she would not hurt him. (3)

8. The Virgin of Guadalupe is the_____ of the Indians because she promised to protect them. (4)

9. Because the bishop did not believe the story, his face had an

   _____ expression. (5)

10. _____ are people who secretly follow someone and
    watch what he does. (8)

11. A person who is _____ ill is very sick. (10)

12. If the Virgin _____ him by talking, he would be too
    late. (10)

13. It was a _____ to Juan to find the roses growing on
    the hill because he knew it was impossible for roses to grow there. (11)

14. She looked like an Indian woman because of her features and her dark

   _____. (15)

3. Synonyms: Replace the underlined word or words with the correct synonym. Choose
from the following list:

> **constructed, pondered over, trail, mound, startled, amazed, desolate,
> serene, approaching, indicated, consider, reflected, miraculous, brief,
> consolation**

1. He passed a small hill on his way to Mass. (2)
2. No one liked stopping at the spot because it was such a lonely
   place. (2)
3. He was shocked when he heard music coming from a mountain. (2)
4. He gave serious thought to what he had seen. (5)
5. After the short visit with the lady, he went to see the bishop. (5)
6. The bishop did not understand why the Holy Mother would
   think of using a poor Indian. (7)
7. She thought a moment and then spoke to him. (9)
8. He watched her coming nearer. (11)
9. The garden of roses was a marvelous sight. (11)
10. He walked down the path on his way to the house of the
    bishop. (12)
11. She had a calm, peaceful appearance. (15)
12. The bishop was surprised when he saw the picture of the Vir-
    gin. (12)
13. The shrine was built in three months. (19)
14. The Virgin had pointed out to Juan where she wanted her
    church built. (19)
15. The people go to the shrine to seek comfort. (20)

4. Antonyms: Choose the word in parentheses that completes each sentence appropriately.

1. To learn to speak one's (native/foreign) language takes very little effort.
2. The parents (bade/forbade) their children to smoke.
3. The moon (disappeared/appeared) behind the clouds.
4. In spite of her calm expression, it was (plain/unclear) to everyone that she was very angry.
5. She was (elated/depressed) by the good news.
6. The small child could not sleep by himself because he was (terrified/unafraid) of the dark.
7. Although he had no proof, we were (convinced/unconvinced) that he spoke the truth.
8. Most of the town had been (saved/destroyed) by the bombing.
9. She always feels (depressed/exhilarated) after a good game of tennis.
10. The Indians of North and South America were (subjugated/liberated) by the Europeans.

5A. Word Formation: When necessary, look for where the words given in the table on page 103 occur in the story. Try to determine meaning from context.

5B. Complete the following sentences with the correct form of the given word.

wonder   1. The music was _____ beautiful.

mistaken   2. There was not a single _____ on the paper.

kindness   3. Her _____ expression consoled him.

protect   4. The mother was too _____ of her children.

dedication   5. To whom did they _____ the shrine?

brilliance   6. The _____ light was almost blinding.

venerate   7. The Chinese hold their ancestors in great
_____ .

assure   8. He gave us his _____ that he would be there on time.

approaching   9. With the _____ of winter, the horses' coats grew longer.

obey   10. The child was punished because he had been
_____ .

PARTICIPLE	NOUN	VERB	ADJECTIVE	ADVERB
wondered wondering	wonder wonderment	wonder	wondrous (2) wonderful	wondrously wonderfully
mistaken mistaking	mistake	mistake	mistaken mistakable unmistakable (7)	mistakenly
	kindness kindliness (3)		kind	kindly
protected protecting	protection protector protectress (4)	protect	protective	protectively
dedicated (13) dedicating	dedication dedicator	dedicate		
obeyed obeying	obedience disobedience	obey (11) disobey	obedient disobedient	obediently disobediently
	brilliance brilliancy		brilliant	brilliantly (14)
venerated venerating	veneration (16)	venerate	venerable	venerably
approached approaching (11)	approach approachableness	approach	approachable	
assured (3) assuring	assurance	assure	assured	assuredly

6. Two-Word Verbs and Verbs-plus-Prepositions: Insert the adverbial particle or preposition that best completes each sentence in the blank provided.

1. He looked _____ to see who was coming down the mountain. (3)

2. He pondered _____ all the things she had told him. (5)

3. At first the priests did not listen _____ Juan. (5)

4. Juan had been sent _____ by the bishop because he did not believe his story. (5)

5. Juan went _____ the mound. (6)

6. They thought the boy was possessed _____ evil spirits. (8)

7. The spies said he was guilty _____ lying. (8)

8. He set _____ right away in order to find a priest. (10)

9. The uncle was healed _____ his illness. (11)

10. Since he took the same route every day, Juan was well acquainted _____ the area. (11)

11. Juan gathered _____ all the roses. (12)

12. He started _____ for the bishop's house. (12)

13. The roses were the proof _____ the Virgin's miraculous appearance. (13)

14. The shrine is dedicated _____ the Virgin of Guadalupe. (13)

7. Idioms and Special Expressions: Find the expressions in the story that match the following phrases:

1. close to dying (10)
2. came closer (4)
3. for certain (9)
4. People quickly found out. (18)
5. decided what needed to be done and saw that it was done (19)
6. always (4)

8. Structure: Past Perfect

"He **was** much depressed, for the Spaniards **had destroyed**
    simple past   *past perfect*

the temple of Tonantzin."

The past perfect is used to express the time relationship between two actions in the past. The action that occurs first is written in the past perfect. The action that follows is in the simple past. (First the Spaniards destroyed the temple. Then he became depressed.)

8A: Fill in the blanks with either the simple past or the past perfect of the verb in parentheses.

Example: He (cross) _____ himself for he (acquire) _____ this custom.

    He crossed himself for he had acquired this custom.

1. The legend (begin) _____ in 1531, only ten years after the Spanish (subjugate) _____ the Valley of Mexico.

2. He (tell) _____ her that the bishop (not believe) _____ him.

3. They (return) _____ to the bishop and told him what (happen) _____ .

4. Not knowing what (happen) _____ , Juan (continue) _____ to the place where he (meet) _____ the Virgin.

5. He (report) _____ that the bishop (command) _____ him to return with some definite token.

6. He (not go) _____ far, however, when he (see) _____ her approaching.

7. She (tell) _____ him not to worry, for at that moment his uncle (be healed) _____ of his sickness.

8. He (take) _____ only a few steps when he (hear) _____ a strange sound.

9. He (see)_____ that the Virgin (disappear)

_____ .

10. It (be)_____ at once clear to the bishop that no

human hands (do)_____ this.

11. They (visit)_____ the spot where the Virgin (speak)

_____ to him.

9. Reading Comprehension: Circle the letter in front of the phrase that best completes each sentence.

1. The Spanish conquered Mexico in
   a. 1531.
   b. 1521.
   c. 1541.
2. Juan Diego was depressed because
   a. he still wasn't a Christian.
   b. he had offended a Christian goddess.
   c. he wasn't sure if accepting Christianity was the right thing to have done.
3. Juan Diego saw the Virgin
   a. three times.
   b. five times.
   c. four times.
4. The second time Juan saw the Virgin was on a
   a. Sunday.
   b. Saturday.
   c. Friday.
5. The two spies thought Juan Diego was possessed of the devil because
   a. he had disappeared so suddenly and could not be found anywhere.
   b. they saw him talking to a strange lady.
   c. he was guilty of witchcraft.
6. The Virgin performed.
   a. one miracle.
   b. several miracles.
   c. no miracles.
7. Juan Diego was amazed to see roses growing on the hill because
   a. it was too cold.
   b. only desert plants grew on the hill.
   c. it was the wrong season for roses.

8. The bishop believed Juan Diego's story when he saw
   a. the brook.
   b. the Virgin herself.
   c. the image of the Virgin.
9. The shrine of the Virgin of Guadalupe is
   a. in Spain.
   b. in the cathedral of Mexico City.
   c. on the hill of Tepeyac.
10. The Virgin of Guadalupe is a special saint for the Mexican Indians because
    a. she appeared to an Indian and looked like an Indian herself.
    b. the bishop declared her to be the protectress of the Indians.
    c. she introduced Christianity to the Indians.

10A. Controlled Writing Practice: Write seven sentences. In each sentence use one of the two-word verbs given below. Model your sentences on those used in the story and on those used in Exercise 6.

look up, ponder over, went up, set off, gather up, send away, start off

10B. Without referring to the story, combine each of the following groups of sentences into one sentence. Then compare your sentence to the sentence in the story.

1. a. An Indian lived in the village of Totpetlac.
   b. He had recently been baptized.
   c. He had changed his name from Quauhtlatohua to Juan Diego.
2. a. Juan was startled and terrified to hear beautiful strains of wondrous music.
   b. The music was coming from the mountainside.
3. a. He automatically crossed himself for he had acquired this custom.
   b. He looked up from the trail.
   c. He beheld a strange sight.
4. a. The bishop was still unconvinced.
   b. He thought the Holy Mother would not consider using such a poor Indian.
   c. He told the man that he must bring some unmistakable token.
5. a. He did not know what had happened.
   b. Juan continued to the place where he had met the Virgin.
6. a. He feared that if he again met the lady, he would be delayed.
   b. He took another route around the hill of Tepeyac.

7. a. He gathered the flowers.
    b. He wrapped them in the folds of his cloak.
    c. He returned down the hill.
8. a. The amazed bishop realized that he had witnessed a miracle.
    b. He fell to his knees in veneration of the Virgin.
    c. He then arose and placed the sacred cloak in the oratory.
9. a. They were guided by the Indian.
    b. They visited the spot where the Virgin had spoken to him.
    c. There the bishop and the priests prayed to the Virgin.
10. a. The people continued to visit the shrine.
    b. The Spaniards called it *Our Lady of Guadalupe.*
    c. To the Indian it was *La Virgen India de Tepeyac.*

11. Topics for Discussion and Writing

A. In most religions, the deity is expressed in masculine terms. Do you think there is also a need for feminine influence? If so, in what ways do Gwan Yin and the Virgin of Guadalupe satisfy this need?

B. Why do you think there were so many conversions to Christianity after the appearance of the Virgin?

C. Do you think religion is an important part of one's cultural identification? Why or why not? What other influences contribute to that identification?

The Hare-Mark on the Moon

SELECTION 11

The Hare-Mark on the Moon

This story is from the Jataka Tales. These ancient Indian tales are stories about the previous lives of Buddha.

city in North India/ animal similar to a rabbit but with long ears/ give religious advice/ advising or urging strongly/ money, food, clothing given to the poor/ to make an offering of something/ Buddhist name for the Hindu God of Thunder, Indra/a Hindu priest

1   Once upon a time, when Brahmadatta was king of Benares, the future Buddha was born as a hare and lived in a wood. He had three friends: a monkey, a jackal, and an otter; all these animals were very wise. The hare used to preach to the others, exhorting them to give alms and keep the fast days by giving food away to those in need. On one of these fast days, the hare and his friends were seeking their food as usual. The otter found some fish, the jackal some meat, and the monkey some mangoes. But the hare reflected that if anyone should ask him for a gift of food, grass would be useless. As he had no grain or meat, he made up his mind to sacrifice his body if anyone asked him for food.

2   Now when any wonderful thing such as this takes place on earth, the throne of Sakra in Heaven grows hot. Sakra looked down to see what was happening and, perceiving the hare, determined to test his virtue. He took the shape of a Brahman and went first to the otter and asked him for food. The otter offered him fish. The jackal and the monkey in turn offered him meat and fruit. Sakra declined all these offers and said that he would return the next day. Then he went to the hare, who was overjoyed at the chance of giving himself in alms. "Brahman," said he, "today I will give such alms as I never gave before; gather wood and prepare a fire and tell me when it is ready." When Sakra heard this, he made a heap of live coals and told the hare that all was ready; then the hare, who would some day be a Buddha, came and sprang into the fire, as

a pinkish bird with long legs that lives near the water/ landing/ unrecognized

happy as a flamingo alighting on a bed of waterlilies. But the fire did not burn—it seemed as cold as the air above the clouds. At once the hare inquired of the disguised Sakra what this meant. Sakra replied that he was not a Brahman but had come down from heaven to test the hare's generosity. The hare answered that he would always be willing to give himself totally.

3   Then Sakra said, "Let your virtue be proclaimed to the end of the world." And taking a mountain, he squeezed it, and holding the hare under his arm, he drew an outline picture of him on the

Adapted from *Myths of the Hindus and Buddhists*, Ananda L. Coomaraswamy and Sister Nivedita (New York: Dover Publications, 1967).

moon, using the juice of the mountain for his ink. Then he put down the hare on some tender grass in the wood and departed to his heaven. And that is why there is now a hare on the moon.

1. Meaning from Context: Fill in the blanks with the appropriate word. Choose from the list given below. When necessary, refer to the story to help determine meaning. The numbers in parentheses in this exercise and all that follow refer to the paragraph in the story where the word appears.

mango, live, fast, inquired, bed, otter, jackals, disguised, heap, alighted, preaching, squeezing

1. He kept the _____ day and gave away his food to the poor. (1)

2. By _____ to the people, the priest helped them lead good lives. (1)

3. The fruit the monkey gave to the Brahman was a

   _____ . (1)

4. An _____ is an animal that lives near water and eats fish. (1)

5. A fire will not start unless the coals are put in a

   _____ . (2)

6. They put out the _____ coals with water. (2)

7. The hare did not recognize Sakra because he was

   _____ . (2)

8. The ducks _____ on the water in search of food. (2)

9. The _____ of flowers was well cared for by the gardener. (2)

10. He _____ of us what the announcement meant, but since we hadn't heard it, we were unable to answer him. (2)

11. _____ are wild dogs that live in Asia and eat meat. (1)

12. She made a pitcher of fresh orange juice by _____ a dozen oranges. (3)

2. Synonyms:
Replace the underlined word or words with the appropriate synonym from the following list:

took place, exhorted, reflected, perceived, declined, alms, determined, seeking, grew, proclaimed

1. The hare urged the others to fast. (1)
2. They gave offerings to the poor. (1)
3. He thought that his offering was useless. (1)
4. Sakra made up his mind to test the hare's virtue. (2)
5. He noticed the hare in the wood. (2)
6. He refused the animals' offers of food. (2)
7. The otter was looking for fish. (1)
8. A wonderful thing happened. (2)
9. The hare's virtue was declared by the god. (3)
10. The throne became hot. (2)

3. Antonyms:
Choose the word in parentheses that completes each sentence appropriately.

1. He was disliked because of his many (virtues/vices).
2. After the picnic they (scattered/gathered) the hot coals in order to put out the fire.
3. The exercise was (useless/useful) because it didn't teach us anything.
4. People asked the advice of the (wise/foolish) old man.
5. They (accepted/declined) the invitation because they were going to another party.
6. A baby's skin is (tough/tender).
7. World War II is part of (modern/ancient) history.
8. He (returned to/forsook) his homeland, but he always longed for it.

4A. Word Formation:
When necessary, look for where the words given in the table on page 113 occur in the story. Try to determine meaning from context.

PARTICIPLE	NOUN	VERB	ADJECTIVE	ADVERB
lived living	life	live	live (2) livable lively	lively
reflected reflecting	reflection reflectiveness	reflect (1)	reflective	
offered offering	offer offering	offer (2)		
determined determining	determination	determine (2)	determinable determinative	
disguised (2) disguising	disguise disguiser	disguise		
answered answering	answer	answer (2)	answerable	
departed departing	departure	depart (3)		
	virtue (2) virtuousness		virtuous	virtuously
	generosity (2) generousness		generous	generously
perceived perceiving (2)	perception	perceive	perceptive	perceptively

4B. Complete the following sentences with the correct form of the given word.

determined   1. He is known for his _____ .

reflect   2. After much _____ they decided to leave their country.

answer   3. She was _____ my question when the phone rang.

using   4. The _____ of this room is allowed only for teachers.

offering   5. He _____ to come and help us.

perceived   6. He has an inaccurate _____ of the problem.

virtue   7. By giving to the poor she acted _____ .

depart   8. We could scarcely see the _____ train.

generous   9. Please give _____ .

life   10. It was a _____ discussion.

5. Literary Style: Ellipsis

"The otter found some fish, the jackal some meat, the monkey some mangoes."

Ellipsis is a process whereby portions of a sentence are deleted. This process occurs frequently in English, and the native reader knows automatically what the missing words are. In the above sentence the verb *found* is deleted twice.

5A. Rewrite each sentence in this exercise by including the elliptical portion.

Example: The otter offered some fish, the jackal meat, and the monkey fruit.

Rewrite: The otter offered some fish, the jackal offered some meat, and the monkey offered some fruit.

1. The turtle said, "In seven days we shall see the earth once again." And so they did.
2. "I myself don't have such a medicine to give you, but I think I know someone who does."
3. Another said, "I have lost my slave." And others, "We have lost our parents."

4. "She is not dead, but asleep."

5. "What animal is that which in the morning goes on four feet, at noon on two feet, and in the evening on three feet?"

6. The wife called her servant and told her to peel the apple. The servant did so.

7. "If you like our music and want us to keep playing, we'll do so."

8. "Let her come upon three horses—one white, one red, one black."

9. "Do you remember," Peel asked "when we stopped at an inn?" She answered, "Of course I do."

10. In one hand he carried a stick of gnarled wood; in the other, a peach.

6. Reading Comprehension: Mark T (true) or F (false) in the blank after each of the following statements.

1. Buddha preached to the animals. _____

2. The animals fasted by giving money to the poor. _____

3. Of the four animals only the hare decided to give himself as food. _____

4. Sakra decided to see if the hare could be true to his decision. _____

5. The animals offered Sakra food because they knew he was a god. _____

6. The Brahman refused the monkey's offer of meat. _____

7. The hare leaped into the fire that the priest had built. _____

8. When the hare jumped into the fire, a flamingo alighted on a bed of waterlilies. _____

9. The fire did not burn because the air was very cold. _____

10. We can see the hare in the moon because Sakra took him up to the moon and put him there on some tender grass. _____

11. The outline of the hare is on the moon so that the world will always remember his generosity. _____

7. Controlled Writing Practice: Combine each group of sentences into a single coherent sentence. Do not refer to the story. After writing the sentences, compare your version with the story's version.

1. The hare used to preach to the others. He exhorted them to give alms and keep the fast days.
2. He had no grain or meat. He therefore made up his mind to give up his body.
3. Sakra looked down. He wanted to see what was happening. He perceived the hare. He determined to test his virtue.
4. He went to the hare. The hare was overjoyed at the chance of giving himself in alms.
5. Sakra heard this. He then made a heap of live coals. He told the hare that all was ready.
6. He took a mountain. He squeezed it. He held the hare under his arm. He drew an outline picture on the moon. He used the juice of the mountain for his ink.

8. Topics for Discussion and Writing

A. Retell the story in your own words.
B. In modern times, are there people who choose a sacrifice similar to the hare's in order to benefit others? Give some examples. Who has done it? Why has he or she done it? What kind of sacrifice have they chosen?
C. Do people in your country fast at certain times? If so, when do they fast? What must they not eat? Why do they fast?

The Sun God
and the Moon God

SELECTION 12

The Sun God and the Moon God

The Mexicans also see a rabbit in the moon. This story explains how their rabbit arrived there.

an early Indian civilization/ periods of time/ flood/flooded

1   According to ancient Toltec legend, the universe passed through four cycles. The end of the fourth cycle was caused by a deluge that completely submerged the earth and destroyed the sun and the moon. The gods lifted the earth up out of the water, but there was still no light. Therefore, a great council of the gods was called to consider what should be done to restore light to the world.

meeting

2   One of them spoke. "It is necessary that we make a new sun and a new moon, and it follows that one of us should be converted into a sun and another into a moon, that there may forever be a god of the sun and a god of the moon."

changed

Another replied, "That is good. But first, how is this to be accomplished, and second, which two of us shall become the gods who shall light the world?"

3   It was decided after much discussion that the two who were to be selected should be cast into a great fire and consumed, from which they would emerge as the gods of light. The second question was more difficult to solve and for many days the discussion continued.

chosen/ thrown/ destroyed/ come out

4   At last the young, rich, and noble Tecuhciztecatl* stepped forward and said, "I am ready to make the sacrifice that the world may be lighted by day."

The other gods nodded in approval. But he who was to become the god of the moon remained to be selected.

After much time had passed, Ranahuantzin,* a god of great homeliness and much poverty, came to the foreground. It was obvious to all the gods that Ranahuantzin's body was filled with fear and that his mind was in terror at the prospect of passing through the fire and being consumed. But it was also clear to them that his soul was filled with compassion for all the men of the world who were without light, and after a brief consultation the group

not handsome; plain/stepped forward/ thought

Adapted from *Of The Night Wind's Telling: Legends from the Valley of Mexico,* by E. Adams Davis. Copyright 1946 by the University of Oklahoma Press.

*In oral reading it might be easier to refer to the two gods as *God T* and *God R*.

accepted him to become the god who would light the world by night.

5   The <u>conclave</u> continued and plans were made for the ceremony by which Tecuhciztecatl and Ranahuantzin were to be converted into the gods of day and night. Two great <u>pyramids</u> were built, the larger and higher of which was to be the home of the god of the day. A great tower was constructed, and on its top a great fire was lighted.

6   Four days before the ceremony of the transformation, Tecuhciztecatl and Ranahuantzin <u>withdrew</u> from the group to do <u>penance</u> in preparation for the sacrifice, and at the end of the period they presented to the fire the offerings that they had collected. Tecuhciztecatl, being a wealthy god, brought gifts of fine quality—beautiful feathers, precious stones, incense, and rare fruits still fresh with dew. The eyes of the other gods brightened with pleasure as they looked upon these gifts. But Ranahuantzin, being a very poor god, brought only green <u>reeds</u> from the <u>marshes</u>, fresh vegetables, sheaves of grass, and thorns that had been dipped in his own blood. The gods remarked to themselves that however ugly and poor Ranahuantzin might be, it was evident that his heart was pure and that he was filled with the desire to serve mankind.

7   When the gifts had been accepted, the two gods withdrew again to their pyramids to meditate and to perform additional acts of penance. Then they dressed themselves for the ceremony. Tecuhciztecatl was clad in rich plumes, with a coat of fine linen cloth and sandals of the finest deer hide, tied with bright colored ribbons. Ranahuantzin had no such <u>finery</u>. He wore a poor headdress and a cloak of crude paper.

8   At the hour of midnight, when the old day dies and the new day is born, the gods assembled at the top of a nearby mountain peak. The wealthy and noble gods were dressed in all their splendor; the lesser and poorer ones in crude headdresses and clothing of paper. A great fire was lit, and soon it blazed so high that the flames almost reached the heavens. Around it sat the gods, with somber countenances, for the hour had come for the <u>ritual</u> that was to <u>create</u> light for the people of the earth.

9   The noblest of the gods <u>arose</u>, raised his hand, and said, "We are ready."

The flames of the great fire leaped even higher. Tecuhciztecatl stood for a moment gazing at them, then <u>dashed</u> toward the flames. But upon reaching the edge, he stopped and backed away, seemingly blinded by the light and fearful of the intense heat. Again, he threw himself toward the flames, and again he stopped short. Was he afraid? Was his spirit not strong enough to make the supreme sacrifice? Twice he had failed. There were two more trials left him. A third time he failed. And a fourth. Tecuhciztecatl hung his head in shame and did not dare meet the startled and angry gaze of the other gods.

meeting

large buildings; base is square, sides slope to a point at the top

went away

self-punishment

tall, thin grasses/soft, wet land

fine clothes

Begin Speed Reading

ceremony

make

stood up

Begin Speed Reading

ran

10   The greatest of the gods arose—his face dark with anger. He pointed to Ranahuantzin, and his voice was as the clap of thunder.

"And now, Ranahuantzin, can you prove yourself?"

The humble god rose to his feet and looked about the circle with a _glance_ that at once sought their permission and _implored_ their encouragement against the fearful _ordeal_ about to be _undertaken_. He squared his shoulders, then launched himself straight into the heart of the flames. There was a crackling, sizzling noise, and Ranahuantzin slowly _disintegrated_ before the eyes of the gods.

look on his face/asked for/difficult trial/done

completely burned up

11   When Tecuhciztecatl saw that the poor god had not failed, he was overcome with shame and, running forward once more, cast himself into the flames.

At that moment a huge eagle flew over the heads of the gods straight into the burning fire, and he was closely followed by a gigantic tiger. The flames leaped and crackled and roared. And around them the gods sat in silence.

12   Gradually the fire _subsided_ and in its very center there appeared two great, golden _disks_, more brilliant than any others the gods had ever seen. Their light was blinding, and their rays of heat burned hot with power to warm all the earth. Light and warmth radiated in all directions and the world began to come alive. Grass began to grow, trees and flowers leaved and blossomed, animals and men stirred as if from a long sleep. The world was a living thing again.

became less intense/ objects in the shape of a flat circle

Then out of the fire flew the eagle, with the disk that was Ranahuantzin in his beak; and after him came the tiger, with the disk that was Tecuhciztecatl held tightly in his claws.

13   But the greatest of the gods said, "It is not right that the light of the sun and the moon be equal."

At that moment a small rabbit that had been attracted to the light ran up to the group. One of the gods picked it up and walked slowly toward the tiger. He glanced inquiringly around the circle, then hurled the rabbit straight into the center of the tiger's disk, the disk that was the noble god Tecuhciztecatl, who had been afraid to enter the fire. With the blow of the rabbit, the countenance of Tecuhciztecatl grew pale, _his radiance diminished_, and he became the moon, while the radiance of the simple-hearted and brave Ranahuantzin continued to glow with all the fiery light of a true sun.

he became less bright

14   Then Quetzalcoatl, the great god of the air, blew a mighty breath. The eagle opened his beak and the sun disk rode away on that mighty breath toward the east, _whence_ he would rise each morning to light the world. And behind him, in lesser brilliance, followed the moon.

from where

And so their _course_ has continued to the present day.

path in the sky

120   *The Sun God and the Moon God*

1. Speed Reading: Read section 9–14 as quickly as you can. Then do the exercise, putting T (true) or F (false) in the blank next to each statement. Do not refer to the story. After completing the exercise, go back and quickly reread the same sections. Again mark T or F in the **second** column. Do not change your first answer and do not refer to the story.

1. At midnight the gods gathered together to watch Tecuhciztecatl and Ranahuantzin offer their gifts.
   _____ _____

2. Tecuhciztecatl tried several times but was at first too afraid to jump into the fire.
   _____ _____

3. After trying several times, Ranahuantzin was finally brave enough to jump into the fire.
   _____ _____

4. Ranahuantzin was burned and then transformed into a shining disk.
   _____ _____

5. Tecuhciztecatl followed Ranahuantzin into the fire.
   _____ _____

6. In the beginning the disks were both equally bright.
   _____ _____

7. The gods decided that the disk in the tiger's claw should be the sun.
   _____ _____

8. The rabbit was thrown at the disk that had been Tecuhciztecatl because he had been afraid to enter the fire.
   _____ _____

9. Ranahuantzin's disk became the moon because it was no longer as bright.
   _____ _____

10. The sun and the moon were set on their course through the sky when the god of the air blew on them.
   _____ _____

2. Meaning from Context: Fill in the blanks with the appropriate word from the list given below. When necessary, refer to the story to help determine meaning. The numbers in parentheses in this exercise and all that follow refer to the section in the story where the word occurs.

blinding, clad, consume, penance, headdresses, additional, conclave, consultation, dew, crude, disintegrated, converted, trials, hide, somber, launched, inquiringly, sheaves, ordeal, precious

1. The meetings of the gods were often happy meetings, but this one was a serious _____ because of the terrible problem. (5)

2. One god offered to be changed into the sun, but still no one wanted to be _____ into a moon. (2)

3. Nothing would be left of the gods because the fire would _____ them. (3)

4. The gods consulted each other. After their _____ , they decided to accept Ranahuantzin. (4)

5. They did _____ in preparation for their sacrifice by fasting for four days. (6)

6. The fruits were still wet with the early morning _____ because they had just been picked. (6)

7. Stones of good quality are called _____ stones. (6)

8. Grasses collected together in bundles are called _____ . (6)

9. The gods had already performed some acts of penance, but the next day they performed _____ acts. (7)

10. One god was dressed in fine clothes, but the other was _____ in only a paper coat. (7)

11. Deer _____ is good leather for shoes and sandals because it is so soft. (7)

12. The rich god's clothes were well made and beautiful, but the poor god's clothes were _____ . (7)

13. The rich gods wore beautiful feathers on their heads, but the _____ of the poor gods were crude. (8)

14. The faces of the gods were not smiling. Instead they were

    _____ because it was such a serious moment. (8)

15. Tecuhciztecatl failed his four_____ , but
    Ranahuantzin passed the first test. (9)

16. The test was an_____ because it was going to be
    very painful. (10)

17. The god_____ into nothing because he was
    consumed by the fire. (10)

18. After Ranahuantzin_____ himself into the fire,
    Tecuhciztecatl decided to throw himself in also. (10)

19. It is difficult to see after looking at the sun because its light is

    _____ . (12)

20. He looked around_____ . The gods answered him by
    nodding their heads. (13)

3. Synonyms: Replace the underlined word or words with the correct synonym. Choose
from the following list:

   **submerged, considered, terror, somber, accomplish, withdrew from,
   cast, period, gaze, implored, countenances, constructed, supreme, obvious, selected, conclave, emerged from, compassion, startled**

 1. After all the rain, the earth was <u>flooded</u>. (1)
 2. They <u>gave serious thought to</u> the difficult problem. (1)
 3. It was an important <u>meeting</u>. (5)
 4. Two gods were <u>chosen</u> to be the sun and the moon. (3)
 5. They had to be <u>thrown</u> into the fire. (3)
 6. They <u>came out of</u> the fire no longer as men but as the sun and
    the moon. (3)
 7. The gods wanted to restore light to the earth, but they were not
    sure how they could <u>achieve</u> this. (2)
 8. It was <u>clear</u> to everybody that the god was afraid. (4)
 9. In spite of his <u>fear</u> of being burned in the fire, he was willing to
    offer himself. (4)
10. He was filled with <u>pity</u> for all the people who were suffering. (4)
11. The gods <u>built</u> two tall pyramids. (5)
12. They <u>left</u> the meeting to prepare for the ceremony. (6)
13. Their <u>time</u> of preparation lasted one week. (6)
14. They were <u>surprised</u> by his unexpected fear. (9)
15. The <u>faces</u> of the gods were unsmiling. Instead they were <u>dark
    and serious</u>. (8)

16. He was embarrassed by their angry <u>look</u>. (9)
17. No other god had been willing to make the <u>perfect</u> sacrifice. (9)
18. He <u>begged</u> for help. (10)

4. Antonyms: Choose the word in parentheses that completes each sentence appropriately.

1. In spite of his great (poverty/wealth), he was not a happy person.
2. We were unable to see clearly the people in the (background/foreground).
3. He was asked to make a (brief/long) speech because the meeting was almost over.
4. In spite of her (homeliness/beauty), she was admired by many people.
5. The boy took the second piece of candy because his mother had nodded her head in (disapproval/approval).
6. In the (pale/brilliant) moonlight we could not see the road clearly.
7. The answer to the problem was (obscure/obvious), but no one thought of it.
8. The crowd (assembled/dispersed) when the soldiers started shooting.
9. They (joined/withdrew from) the group when they saw they were unwanted.
10. These are (precious/worthless) stones, but they look like real diamonds.
11. Silks and satins are expensive, (fine/crude) materials.
12. Although the mountain looked close, it was (far away/nearby).
13. Unless your shoestrings are tied (tightly/loosely), they will come undone.
14. Great wealth and power usually (attract/repel) people.
15. As he became sicker and sicker, his strength (increased/diminished).

5A. Word Formation: When necessary, look for where the words given in the table on page 125 occur in the story. Try to determine meaning from context.

5B. Complete the following sentences with the correct form of the given word.

accomplish   1. For which _____ is he most well known?

PARTICIPLE	NOUN	VERB	ADJECTIVE	ADVERB
accomplished (2) accomplishing	accomplishment	accomplish	accomplishable	
approved approving	approval (4) approver	approve disapprove	approvable	approvingly
collected (6) collecting	collection collector	collect	collective collectible	collectively
withdrawn withdrawing	withdrawal	withdraw (6)		
terrorized terrorizing	terror (4) terrorism terrorist	terrorize	terroristic	
implored imploring		implore (10)		imploringly
sacrificed sacrificing	sacrifice (4) sacrificer	sacrifice	sacrificial	sacrificially
encouraged encouraging	encouragement (10)	encourage	encouraging	encouragingly
disintegrated disintegrating	disintegration disintegrator	disintegrate (10)	disintegrative	
radiated radiating	radiation radiance radiator	radiate (12)	radiant	radiantly

approval	2. She looked_____ at the child.
collect	3. He has a fine art_____ .
withdraw	4. They asked permission to be_____ from school early.
terror	5. The_____ was sentenced to life imprisonment.
implore	6. He_____ his friend's forgiveness.
sacrificed	7. The_____ was offered to the god.
encourage	8. Without the coach's_____ , he would never have succeeded.
disintegrate	9. She threw the letter in the fire and watched as it _____ .
radiant	10. The actress was_____ beautiful.

5C. Find adjectives from the story that can be changed into group nouns for people by putting *the* in front of them. Select the adjectives from the following sections. Write the nouns in the spaces provided. Do not use the same adjective twice.

Example: "... the disk that was the noble god Tecuhciztecatl ..." (13)

adjective: **noble**   group noun: **the noble**

Section 4	_____	_____
	_____	_____
	_____	_____
Section 6	_____	_____
	_____	_____
Section 10	_____	_____
Section 13	_____	_____
	_____	_____

6. Prepositions: Insert the preposition that best completes each sentence in the blank provided.

1. After the world passed _____ its fourth cycle, it was destroyed by a flood. (1)

2. The gods decided that one of them should be converted

   _____ a moon, and another

   _____ a sun. (2)

3. The poor god was filled _____ fear at the thought of
   dying. (4)

4. They withdrew _____ the meeting. (6)

5. The gods presented _____ the fire their offerings. (6)

6. The gods were dressed _____ fine clothes. (8)

7. He was overcome _____ shame when he saw the
   bravery of Ranahuantzin. (11)

8. After failing four times he hung his head _____
   shame. (9)

9. The rabbit was attracted _____ the fire. (13)

10. Holding a rabbit, the god walked _____ the tiger. (13)

7. Word Association

7A. The words in the box are associated with the idea of fire. Complete the paragraph
using each word only once.

flames	blaze	lit	leaped
roaring	sizzling	subsided	crackling

The gods gathered wood for the fire. When it was time for

the ceremony, they _____ it. The

_____ grew hotter and hotter. They

_____ high in the air. The fire continued to

_____ for a long time. Its

_____ and _____

could be heard from far away. Finally it

_____ and only a few hot coals were left.
Water was poured on them to put them out. At first there was the

smell of smoke and the sound of _____ ,
and then the fire was completely out.

7B. These words have a religious connotation. Again, fill in the blanks of the following paragraph using each word only once.

ceremony	penance	holy	worship
ritual	meditate	offering	sacrifice

Every year at this time the Indians have a religious

_____ . They come together at a

_____ shrine to

_____ their gods. First, they do

_____ for their sins by praying and fasting.

Next, they _____ by thinking about their

past life. They then make a _____ to the

gods. The sacrifice is usually an _____ of

food. Year after year, the _____ is always
the same.

7C. These words are associated with the idea of the sun. Fill in the blanks of the following paragraph using each word only once.

glow	light	blinding	fiery
brilliance	rays	radiated	

The _____ _____ of the

sun _____ in all directions. Its

_____ warmed the entire earth. Everyone
felt it, but no one could look at it because of its

_____ _____ . Even

after it had set in the west, its _____ could
still be seen.

8. Reading Comprehension: Circle the letter in front of the phrase that best completes each sentence.

1. There was no light on earth
   a. during the first four cycles of the world.
   b. at the end of the fourth cycle.
   c. because the sun and the moon had not yet been created.

2. A meeting was held to discuss
   a. how to end the flood.
   b. how to restore light to the world.
   c. how to choose a new leader of the gods.

3. The second question was more difficult to solve because the gods didn't know
   a. who would be willing to offer themselves.
   b. how to make a new sun and a new moon.
   c. which of the two volunteers should be the sun.

4. Tecuhciztecatl was chosen to be the god of the day because he was
   a. the bravest.
   b. rich and noble.
   c. afraid.

5. The Indians believed
   a. all their gods were equal.
   b. all their gods were perfect.
   c. some gods had more power and wealth than others.

6. The gods
   a. admired Ranahuantzin.
   b. disliked him because of his poverty and homeliness.
   c. made fun of him.

7. When the greatest of the gods spoke to Ranahuantzin,
   a. his voice was loud and angry.
   b. there was thunder in the sky.
   c. he clapped his hands.

8. Before running toward the fire, Ranahuantzin
   a. bent over to get a better start.
   b. looked away from the other gods.
   c. stood up straight.

9. Ranahuantzin became the god of the sun because
   a. the rabbit landed by chance on the tiger's disk.
   b. the rabbit landed on the eagle's disk.
   c. he had been the greater of the two gods.

10. The sun and the moon were restored to the world because
   a. the eagle and the tiger sacrificed themselves.
   b. two gods had made the supreme sacrifice.
   c. Quetzalcoatl blew a mighty breath.

9A. Controlled Writing Practice: Write ten sentences. In each sentence, use one of the phrases given below. Model your sentences on those used in Exercise 6 and those used in the story.

pass through, convert into, be filled with, withdraw from, present to, be dressed in, be overcome with shame, hang his head in shame, be attracted to, walk toward

9B. Put the following sentences in the correct order without looking at the story.

1. He squared his shoulders, then launched himself straight into the heart of the flames.
2. "And now, Ranahuantzin, can you prove yourself?"
3. There was a crackling, sizzling noise, and Ranahuantzin slowly disintegrated before the eyes of the gods.
4. When Tecuhciztecatl saw that the poor god had not failed, he was overcome with shame and, running forward once more, cast himself into the flames.
5. The humble god rose to his feet and looked about the circle with a glance that at once sought their permission and implored their encouragement against the fearful ordeal about to be undertaken.
6. At that moment a huge eagle flew over the heads of the gods straight into the burning fire, and he was closely followed by a gigantic tiger.

9C. Write a summary of the story by completing the following sentences. The first sentence is completed for you. Use a separate piece of paper and write the summary in paragraph form.

   Since the moon and the sun had been destroyed in a great flood, the gods held a meeting to decide how to restore light to the earth. A rich and noble god and a poor and humble god . . .
   The rich god was unable . . .
   but the poor god . . .
   Feeling ashamed the rich god . . .
   Out of the fire came . . .
   One was in the . . .
   The other was in the . . .

Both were equally . . .
Therefore, one of the gods . . .
The disk . . .
That is the reason why . . .

10. Topics for Discussion and Writing

A. In what ways are "The Hare-Mark on the Moon" and "The Sun God and the Moon God" similar? In what ways are they different?

B. In the United States, people see a man in the moon. Do people in your country see a figure in the moon? Can you tell us the story that goes with the figure?

C. The hare and Ranahuantzin achieved a certain kind of immortality in that they are forever remembered. What kind of sacrifice led to this immortality? Can you share any other stories of heroes who insured their immortality in the same way?

D. Compare and contrast Ranahuantzin and Tecuhciztecatl.

The Search for the Land of Bliss

The Search for the Land of Bliss

1   In Vietnam, if a man sees a really beautiful woman he may say, "There is someone so perfect, she must have come from the Land of <u>Bliss</u>!" If so, he will be referring to the ancient tale of Tu Thuc, who once found this <u>Elysium</u>, but returned from it. This is his story.

happiness

place of perfect happiness

2   More than five centuries ago, during the reign of King Tran Thuan Ton, there lived a mandarin named Tu Thuc who was less interested in government and administration than in music, wine, poetry, and nature. Tu Thuc was a dreamer. His book knowledge was vast, but the ancient <u>sages</u> had never told him one thing: the precise location of the Land of Bliss where the Tien, the immortal beings, lived. And this he longed to know. In fact he wanted to visit this spot, for as a child he had been taught that the Land of Bliss was the place discovered by the Chinese Emperor Duong Minh Hoang one autumn evening when viewing the lantern moon. Upon later returning to earth, this emperor had reported that the Land of Bliss was a marvelous place, where everyone possessed eternal youth and passed the time in singing, dancing, laughing, reciting poetry, and feasting. All the women there were radiantly beautiful, he declared, with skin like peach bloom, and they dressed in flowing rainbow-colored robes with sleeves like butterfly wings. They performed the graceful Nghe Thuong dance, which the emperor himself taught to the court ladies at his palace so that he could enjoy watching them while he sipped his perfumed wine in his garden under the full moon.

wise men

3   To live this sort of life in a place like the Land of Bliss seemed extremely attractive to Tu Thuc. But he was now administrator of the district of Tien Du, where he had been <u>posted</u> from his native province of Thanh Hoa. One day he visited an old pagoda near his residence to view a famous peony bush in full bloom. Every year when the bush flowered, its magnificent blossoms attracted a throng of pilgrims. It was now the second month of the year Binh Ti, and the flower festival was at its height. A lovely young girl of perhaps fifteen or sixteen, possessed of a quiet, serene beauty, seemed to be particularly interested in the large red

sent to place of duty

Adapted from *Land of Seagull and Fox: Folk Tales of Vietnam*, Ruth San; Charles E. Tuttle Co., Inc., Tokyo, Japan, publisher.

flowers. Leaning close to them, she lifted a branch to get a closer look. But, suddenly, the branch snapped and broke off in her hand.

4 The pagoda authorities were shocked at what they considered <u>desecration</u> and held the girl to insure compensation. Evening was now coming on, but no one had appeared to pay for the damage and to take the girl home. It was at this time that Tu Thuc happened to come in. Hearing the story, he removed his brocaded outer robe and gave it in exchange for the girl's freedom. She was released and went her way.

using a sacred thing in an unworthy way

5 As the story spread, everyone came to praise the mandarin for his goodness and generosity. But Tu Thuc's heart was less than ever in his official duties. Thus, despite his good reputation among the people, he neglected his office and often <u>incurred</u> the reproaches of the senior mandarins.

brought upon himself

6 Finally, Tu Thuc sadly told himself, "Truly, for just a few scraps of <u>paddy</u> land <u>in lieu</u> of salary why should I stay forever chained to this circle of honors and worldly interests? I'd rather spend the rest of my days wandering the world in a slender <u>skiff</u>, seeking the ends of the <u>limpid</u> waters and the blue mountains. Thus I'd no longer be following a way of life that goes against all the secret desires of my heart."

rice still growing/ instead/ small boat/ clear

7 So it came about that one day Tu Thuc untied the <u>cords</u> of his mandarin <u>seal</u> and returned it to his superiors. Then he retired to the countryside at Tong Son, whose streams and <u>grottoes</u> he loved to explore. His long <u>leisure</u> now permitted him to make many <u>excursions</u>, on each of which he was accompanied by a young boy—half disciple, half servant—who carried his gourd of wine, his moon <u>lute</u>, and a book of poems. Reaching a spot that particularly struck his fancy, Tu Thuc would sit down to drink and strum his lute. Always he sought out picturesque and unusual sites. The Pink Mountain, the Grotto of the Green Clouds, the Lai River, Nga Harbor—Tu Thuc visited them all, and celebrated their beauty in verse.

strings symbol of office/caves

free time/ pleasure trips

stringed musical instrument

8 One morning, after having arisen and set out before daybreak, Tu Thuc saw, several <u>leagues</u> away beside the sea, five clouds of different colors and shifting shapes, which expanded before his eyes, then came together in the shape of a lotus flower. Quickly he went to the spot by boat. There he saw a magnificent mountain, rising from the sea in a place where there never had been a mountain before. He longed to climb it, but the mountain seemed impossibly steep. So he turned back to his boat, filled with regret, and slowly tore himself away to the waiting emptiness.

measure of distance

9 But suddenly he saw the sides of the mountain open wide, as if inviting him to come in. Tu Thuc entered a passageway where the darkness soon became complete. Keeping his hand on the mossy wall of the <u>grotto</u>, he groped his way along a narrow, twisting route. Finally, he saw a light. Raising his eyes, he saw high

cave

above his head an opening. Clinging to the rough edges of rocks, Tu Thuc climbed until he reached a wide path. When he reached the top, the atmosphere was clear, and a lovely, radiant sun was shining.

10   Tu Thuc stood as if enchanted, under blossoms that drifted down like snow. Near his feet a <u>peacock</u> preened its shimmering tail. Then young attendants dressed in blue appeared. Said one to the other, "Here is the young man <u>betrothed</u> to this house; he has already arrived." The attendants disappeared into the principal palace to announce Tu Thuc; then they returned, <u>bowed</u> low before him, and said: "We invite your lordship to enter."

large male bird with beautiful tail feathers/ engaged to be married

bent down at the waist

11   Tu Thuc followed, and ascending a broad staircase, he was led before a woman dressed in white silk who invited him to sit in an armchair of white sandalwood.

12   The woman said, "Learned scholar and lover of picturesque sites, do you know what place you are now in? Do you by chance remember a meeting near a blossoming peony bush?"

13   Tu Thuc replied, "It's true that as a faithful lover of lakes and rivers I've wandered in many places, yet I never knew that there existed a landscape worthy of immortals. I am but a simple man, fond of beauty. I go where my steps lead me, unconcerned about my fate. As for the peony blossoms . . . Dare I ask you to enlighten me?"

14   The woman smiled. "How could you know this place indeed? You are in the sixth of the thirty-six grottoes of Mount Phi Lai, which runs through all the seas without its base ever being touched by the sun. Born of the winds and rains, it is formed and then vanishes according to the <u>whim</u> of the winds. I am the Tien of this grotto and my name is Nguy. I know of the nobility of your nature, Tu Thuc, and know, too, the quality of your soul. So that is why I have welcomed you here. As for the peonies . . ."

sudden desire

15   She turned toward the attendants, who understood her silent command and withdrew. A little later a young girl entered. Looking at her, Tu Thuc recognized the same young lady who had broken the peony branch at the pagoda.

16   The Tien spoke again, "This is my daughter, called Giang Huong, <u>Vermilion</u> Incense. When she went down to earth to the festival of flowers, a misfortune befell her. It was you who came to her rescue. Never have I forgotten this priceless act of kindness. Now, as payment of our debt of gratitude, I permit your two lives to be joined."

bright red

The guardians of all the grottoes were invited to the wedding ceremony, which was celebrated with music and song.

Begin Speed Reading

17   The days and weeks fled away as fast as a weaver's <u>shuttle</u>. The Land of Bliss was eternal springtime, and Tu Thuc felt

instrument used for weaving

there was nothing more he could wish for. Then suddenly, inexplicably, he was seized with longing for the world of dust and sorrow, for the wife and children whom he had left at his native village.

18   Finally he confided to Giang Huong, "My beloved knows that when I came here I had set out only for a morning excursion, and that I have already been gone for a long time. It is difficult to lull forever the human feelings in our hearts, and you must see that I still dream too much about my native village. . . . What do you think of my desire to return sometime to my home?"

19   Giang Huong appeared to hesitate at the idea of a separation. But Tu Thuc pursued the thought, "It would be only a matter of days, of a month at the very most. Let me bring news about myself to my family, to my friends. Everything can be quickly done and I shall return without delay."

20   Weeping, Giang Huong answered, "I will not invoke our love to oppose my husband's desires. But the boundaries of the mortal world are narrow and limited, its days and months very brief. I fear that my husband will not find again the familiar appearance of a time that is ended. Where are the willows of the courtyard and the flowers of the garden?"

21   Later, Giang Huong confided her sorrow to the Grand Tien, her mother, who expressed regret. "I didn't expect to see him still tied to the world of dust and sorrow. But, since he is, let him go then. . . . Why all this grief? He cannot be changed."

22   So, at the moment of farewell, Giang Huong dried her tears and gave Tu Thuc a letter written on silk. She asked him not to open it until he had arrived at his destination. Her husband climbed into a waiting chariot provided by the Tien, and in the twinkling of an eye he was back in his village.

23   Everything now appeared totally different from what he had remembered. The landscape, the houses, the people—all were unfamiliar. Only the stream descending from the mountain seemed as it had been. There was a new bridge spanning it, with strange people hurrying across it, and at a place where Tu Thuc recalled *soft, wet land* only a marshy swamp, there was now a prosperous marketplace. After identifying himself, Tu Thuc made inquiry of some old men passing by.

24   Finally, one of them seemed to remember. "When I was very little," he recalled, "I heard it said that one of my ancestors bore the name you give yourself. He was chief of the Tien Du district. But he resigned his office about a hundred years ago, set off for an *succession of rulers belonging to one family* unknown destination, and never returned. That was toward the end of the Tran dynasty and we are now under the fourth king of the Le dynasty.

25 Tu Thuc then gave an account of his miraculous experience and reckoned that the time he had stayed in the Land of Bliss must have been one hundred days.

26 "I have heard that a day in the Land of Bliss is the same as a year on earth, so probably you are my forebear," said the old man. "Let me show you the old family home."

27 And he led Tu Thuc to a desolate spot where there stood a dilapidated house, totally beyond repair. Feeling very alone and very sad, Tu Thuc now wanted to go back to where he had come from. But the chariot had been transformed into a phoenix, which had wheeled away and disappeared in the sky. Tu Thuc then opened the letter Giang Huong had given him and read these lines:

phoenix
mythical bird often depicted in Chinese painting

> In the midst of the clouds there is centered
> the affection of the phoenix;
> Of yesterday's union this is already the end.
> Above the seas, who seeks traces of the immortals?
> For a future meeting there is no hope.

28 Now Tu Thuc understood that the parting from his beautiful wife would be forever. So later, dressed in a light cloak and with a conical hat on his head, Tu Thuc climbed the Yellow Mountain in the land of Nong Cong, in the province of Thanh Hoa. From there he never returned. It is not known whether he ever succeeded in returning to the kingdom of the Tien, or if he was lost forever on the mountain.

1. Speed Reading: Read sections 18–28 as quickly as you can. Then do the exercise, putting T (true) or F (false) in the blank next to each statement. Do not refer to the story. After completing the exercise, go back and quickly reread the same sections. Again mark T or F in the **second** column. Do not change your first answer and do not refer to the story.

1. The time in the Land of Bliss seemed to pass slowly. _____ _____

2. The beauty of the Land of Bliss kept Tu Thuc from feeling sad or homesick. _____ _____

3. Tu Thuc had left a family behind. _____ _____

4. Tu Thuc wanted to return home forever. _____ _____

5. Giang Huong warned Tu Thuc that the world would look different. _____ _____

6. The mother advised Giang Huong to let him go back. _____ _____

7. No one could remember anything about Tu Thuc. _____ _____

8. Tu Thuc's house was still standing. _____ _____

9. Tu Thuc could not go back to the Land of Bliss because his chariot was broken. _____ _____

10. Tu Thuc has never returned from the Land of Bliss. _____ _____

2. Meaning from Context: Fill in the blanks with the appropriate word from the list given below. When necessary, refer to the story to help determine meaning. The numbers in parentheses in this exercise and all that follow refer to the section in the story where the word appears.

steep, groped, spanning, recite, peony, expands, conical, sipped, compensation, reckoned, strum, skiff, verse, mossy, picturesque, dilapidated

1. He does not sing that well, but he can _____ poetry beautifully. (2)

2. Good wine should be _____ rather than gulped. (2)

3. A _____ is a flower with magnificent blossoms that are sometimes red. (3)

4. Tu Thuc gave his expensive robe as _____ for the damage done to the bush. (4)

5. He sailed away in a _____ looking for the Land of Bliss (6)

6. A balloon _____ when filled with air. (8)

7. To play a guitar one must _____ the strings. (7)

8. Do you find it easier to memorize something written in

_____ or in prose? (7)

9. Most mountains are difficult to climb because they are so

   _____ . (8)

10. The walls of a grotto are often_____ because moss grows where it is damp and dark. (9)

11. While walking in the dark, he_____ his way in order not to fall. (9)

12. Lakes and rivers are usually_____ sites. (12)

13. He looked at his watch and_____ that he had been gone for three hours. (25)

14. Because a bridge is now_____ the river, we can cross over to the other side. (23)

15. The house looked_____ because it had been abandoned for such a long time. (27)

16. If an ice-cream cone is turned upside down, it looks like a small

    _____ hat. (28)

3. Synonyms: Replace the underlined word or words with the correct synonym. Choose from the following list:

> **declared, vast, reproaches, disciples, radiant, sites, autumn, reported, priceless, invoked, excursion, shifting**

1. Because of his <u>immense</u> wealth, he could buy whatever he wanted. (2)
2. Which is your favorite season, spring of <u>fall</u>? (2)
3. The senator <u>announced</u> his decision to resign from office. (2)
4. He <u>related</u> all that he had seen on his travels. (2)
5. In spite of the <u>rebukes</u> he received from his wife, the man still refused to look for a job. (5)
6. Buddha had many <u>followers</u>. (7)
7. The <u>changing</u> shadows were caused by the sun going in and out of the clouds. (8)
8. She always looks happy because of her <u>bright</u> smile. (9)
9. We usually go on an <u>outing</u> every Sunday. (7)
10. There are many beautiful <u>places</u> to visit in Europe. (12)
11. His art collection is <u>invaluable</u>. (16)
12. In asking his brother's forgiveness, he <u>appealed to</u> their ties of blood. (20)

4. Antonyms: Choose the word in parentheses that completes each sentence appropriately.

1. To be (immortal/mortal) is to live forever.
2. He was (released/detained) by the authorities because he did not have proper identification.
3. She was (ascending/descending) the stairs on her way to the basement when the phone rang.
4. She was unable to relax because she was (worried/unconcerned) about her children.
5. The miraculous appearance of the mountain was (explicable/inexplicable).
6. The gentle singing (lulled/agitated) the child.
7. The (forebears/descendants) of the people in the U.S. came from all over the world.
8. Too much (leisure/toil) can make a person lazy.
9. If the student had been less (concerned/indifferent) about the quality of his work, he would have gotten a better grade.
10. Everyone agreed to meet at the (base/summit) of the mountain, so they could climb it together.

5. Literary Style: Match the more formal or literary expressions on the left with the sentences on the right.

a. His heart was not in it.

b. It went against his desires.

c. It struck his fancy.

d. He tore himself away.

e. Misfortune befell him.

f. His steps led him.

g. He sought it out.

h. He came to its rescue.

1. _____ He didn't want to do it.

2. _____ He especially liked it.

3. _____ He looked for it.

4. _____ He had bad luck.

5. _____ He wasn't excited about it.

6. _____ It was very difficult for him to leave.

7. _____ He went without a special goal.

8. _____ He saved it.

i. He went in the   9. _____   He asked them.
   twinkling of an eye.

j. He pursued the   10. _____   He went quickly.
   thought.

k. He made inquiry of   11. _____   He continued with
   them.   his thought.

6A. Word Formation: When necessary, look for where the words given in the table on page 142 occur in the story. Try to determine meaning from context.

6B. Complete the following sentences with the correct form of the given word.

1. Before you start the game, _____ yourself   *familiar*
   with the rules.

2. Would you _____ me on this subject?   *enlightened*

3. The _____ was unsatisfactory.   *explicable*

4. She was _____ with the gift.   *enchant*

5. She was _____ dressed.   *attract*

6. He went in the _____ direction.   *oppose*

7. He is a good ruler, but he lacks _____   *administer*
   ability.

8. Columbus discovered America, but he did not   *explorer*
   _____ it.

9. Many _____ came to the opening of the new   *celebrate*
   theater.

10. Did she _____ when she answered the   *hesitation*
    question?

7. Prepositions: Insert the preposition that best completes each sentence in the blank provided.

1. The mandarin was interested _____ poetry. (2)

2. She was possessed _____ great beauty. (3)

3. Tu Thuc was shocked _____ the sight of his
   dilapidated house. (4)

PARTICIPLE	NOUN	VERB	ADJECTIVE	ADVERB
familiarized / familiarizing	familiarity / familiarization	familiarize	familiar (20)	familiarly
enlightened / enlightening	enlightenment	enlighten (13)		
explained / explaining	explanation	explain	explanatory / explicable / inexplicable	inexplicably (17)
enchanted (10) / enchanting	enchantment / enchanter	enchant / disenchant		enchantingly
attracted / attracting	attraction / attractiveness	attract	attractive (3) / unattractive / attractable	attractively
opposed / opposing	opposition / opposer	oppose (20)	opposite	
administrated / administrating	administration (2) / administrator	administrate	administrative	administratively
explored / exploring	explorer / exploration	explore (7)	exploratory	
celebrated (16) / celebrating	celebration / celebrity	celebrate		
hesitated / hesitating	hesitation / hesitance	hesitate (19)	hesitant	hesitantly / hesitatingly

4. He would travel to many lovely places _____ boat. (8)

5. The girl was dressed entirely _____ white. (10)

6. Tu Thuc did not know whether the girl had come to the festival
_____ chance or on purpose. (12)

7. Tu Thuc was unconcerned _____ his future. (13)

8. His generous act was worthy _____ praise. (13)

9. He did not wish _____ worldly honors. (17)

10. She confided her troubles _____ her mother. (18)

11. He could no longer live in his house because it was
_____ repair. (27)

12. He succeeded _____ finding his way out of the
grotto. (28)

8. Reading Comprehension: Circle the letter in front of the phrase that best completes
each sentence.

1. The Emperor Duong Minh Hoang lived
   a. five centuries ago.
   b. during the reign of King Tran Thuan Ton.
   c. before Tu Thuc.
2. The authors of Tu Thuc's books never mentioned
   a. the Land of Bliss.
   b. where the Land of Bliss was exactly located.
   c. where the Tien could be found.
3. The young girl broke the peony branch because
   a. she wanted to desecrate the pagoda.
   b. she wanted Tu Thuc to notice her.
   c. She wanted to look at it closely because of its beauty.
4. To break the peony branch was considered desecration
   because
   a. the pagoda was a religious place.
   b. the flower festival was at its height.
   c. the flower was beautiful.
5. The senior mandarins were upset with Tu Thuc because
   a. of his good reputation among the people.
   b. he neglected his official duties.
   c. he had come to the girl's aid.

6. Tu Thuc was able to do whatever he wanted because
   a. he had resigned his office.
   b. the authorities had fired him.
   c. of his big salary.

7. The beautiful mountain Tu Thuc discovered
   a. was a place of pilgrimage.
   b. was the Land of the Immortals.
   c. consisted of six grottoes.

8. Tu Thuc was allowed to marry Giang Huong because
   a. it was she whom he had rescued at the flower festival.
   b. he had desired to find the Land of Bliss.
   c. he was now an immortal.

9. Tu Thuc wanted to return home because
   a. there was nothing more he could wish for.
   b. he no longer loved Giang Huong.
   c. he was homesick for his former family.

10. Giang Huong asked him to stay because
    a. of their love for each other.
    b. she knew he would be disappointed if he went.
    c. the Grand Tien expressed regret.

11. "Where are the willows of the courtyard and the flowers of the garden?"
    This question, asked by Giang Huong, refers to
    a. her wish that Tu Thuc bring her some flowers and some willows.
    b. the fact that nothing would look the same on earth.
    c. the end of the spring.

12. King Tran Tuan Ton lived
    a. during the Le dynasty.
    b. near the end of the Tran dynasty.
    c. a hundred years before Tu Thuc.

13. Time in the Land of Bliss went
    a. more slowly than in the world of mortals.
    b. more quickly than in the land of mortals.
    c. a hundred times faster than in the land of mortals.

14. Tu Thuc could not return to the Land of Bliss because
    a. his chariot had disappeared in the sky.
    b. his chariot had turned into a bird.
    c. he had forgotten to open the letter.

9A. Controlled Writing Practice: Write twelve sentences using the phrases given on page 145. Model your sentences on those used in Exercise 7 and those used in the story.

interested in, possessed of, shocked at, wish for, succeed in, travel by, dressed in, by chance, unconcerned about, worthy of, confide to, beyond repair.

9B. Review with your teacher the meanings of the following transition markers:

for example, consequently, nevertheless, thus, furthermore, subsequently

9C. Complete the following pairs of sentences using your own words:

1. Tu Thuc was a dreamer. Furthermore,

_____ .

2. Tu Thuc neglected his duties. Consequently,

_____ .

3. Tu Thuc loved the outdoors. For example,

_____ .

4. The mountain was too steep to climb. Thus,

_____ .

5. In the beginning, Tu Thuc was very happy in the Land of Bliss. Subsequently,

_____ .

6. Tu Thuc loved Giang Huong. Nevertheless,

_____ .

7. Giang Huong thought he would be disappointed if he returned to earth. Yet,

_____ .

8. Tu Thuc expected to see his family and friends. Instead,

_____ .

9. Tu Thuc knew that he would never see his wife again. Furthermore,

_____ .

10. Tu Thuc wanted to return to the Land of Bliss. However,

_____ .

10. Topics for Discussion and Writing

A. Describe the personality of Tu Thuc. Give examples from the story to support your description.

B. Why did Tu Thuc say that the land he had left behind was "a world of dust and sorrow"? (paragraph 17)

C. Reread the descriptions of the Land of Bliss (paragraphs 2, 10, 14). Then write your own description of a "Land of Bliss."

One Night in Paradise

One Night in Paradise

The following folk tale is an Italian version of a "short" visit to the Land of Bliss.

1   Once upon a time there were two close friends who, out of affection for each other, made this pledge: the first to get married would call on the other to be his <u>best man</u>, even if he should be at the ends of the earth.

bridegroom's friend who attends him at the wedding

2   Shortly thereafter one of the friends died. The survivor, who was planning to get married, had no idea what he should now do, so he sought the advice of his <u>confessor</u>.

priest to whom people confess and go for advice

"This is a ticklish situation," said the priest, "but you must keep your promise. Call on him even if he is dead. Go to his grave and say what you're supposed to say. It will then be up to him whether to come to your wedding or not."

The youth went to the grave and said, "Friend, the time has come for you to be my best man."

The earth yawned, and out jumped the friend. "By all means. I have to keep my word, or else I'd end up in <u>Purgatory</u> for no telling how long."

place after death where one suffers temporarily

3   They went home, and from there to church for the wedding. Then came the wedding banquet, where the dead youth told all kinds of stories, but not a word did he say about what he'd witnessed in the next world. The bridegroom longed to ask him some questions, but he didn't have the nerve. At the end of the banquet the dead man rose and said, "Friend, since I've done you this favor, would you walk me back a part of the way?"

"Why, certainly! But I can't go far, naturally, since this is my wedding night."

"I understand. You can turn back any time you like."

4   The bridegroom kissed his bride. "I'm going to step outside for a moment, and I'll be right back." He walked out with the dead man. They chatted about first one thing and then another, and before you knew it, they were at the grave. There they embraced,

and the living man thought, if I don't ask him now, I'll never ask him." He therefore took heart and said, "Let me ask you something since you are dead. What's it like in the hereafter?"

"I really can't say," answered the dead man. "If you want to find out, come along with me to Paradise."

5   The grave opened, and the living man followed the dead one inside. Thus they found themselves in Paradise. The dead man took his friend to a handsome crystal palace with gold doors, where angels played their harps for blessed souls to dance, with St. Peter strumming the double bass. The living man gaped at all the splendor, and goodness knows how long he would have remained in the palace if there hadn't been all the rest of Paradise to see. "Come on to another spot now," said the dead man, who led him into a garden whose trees, instead of foliage, displayed song birds of every color. "Wake up, let's move on!" said the dead man, guiding his visitor onto a lawn where <u>angels</u> danced as joyously and gracefully as lovers. "Next we'll go to see a star!" He could have gazed at the stars forever. Instead of water, their rivers ran with wine, and their land was of cheese.

immortal beings often depicted with wings

6   All of a sudden, he started. "Oh my goodness, friend, it's later than I thought. I have to get back to my bride, who's surely worried about me."

"Have you had enough of Paradise so soon?"

"Enough? If I had my choice . . ."

"And there's still so much to see!"

"I believe you, but I'd better be getting back."

"Very well, suit yourself." The dead man walked him back to the grave and vanished.

7   The living man stepped from the grave, but no longer recognized the cemetery. It was packed with monuments, statues, and tall trees. He left the cemetery and saw huge buildings in place of the simple stone cottages that used to line the streets. The streets were full of automobiles and streetcars, while airplanes flew through the skies. "Where on earth am I? Did I take the wrong street? And look how these people are dressed!" He stopped a little old man on the street. "Sir, what is this town?"

8   "This city, you mean."

"All right, this city. But I don't recognize it, for the life of me. Can you please direct me to the house of the man who got married yesterday?"

"Yesterday? I happen to be the <u>sacristan</u>, and I can assure you no one got married yesterday!"

person who takes care of a church

"What do you mean? I got married myself!" Then he gave an account of accompanying his dead friend to Paradise.

"You're dreaming," said the old man. "That's an old story people tell about the bridegroom who followed his friend into the grave and never came back, while his bride died of sorrow."

"That's not so, I'm the bridegroom myself!"

Christian priest of high rank
"Listen, the only thing for you to do is to go and speak with our bishop."

division of a county with its own church and priest
"Bishop? But here in town there's only the parish priest."

"What parish priest? For years and years we've had a bishop." And the sacristan took him to the bishop.

9   The youth told his story to the bishop, who recalled an event he'd heard about as a boy. He took down the parish books and began flipping back the pages. Thirty years ago, no. Fifty years ago, no. One hundred, no. Two hundred, no. He went on thumbing the pages. Finally on a yellowed, crumbling page he put his finger on those very names. "It was three hundred years ago. The young man disappeared from the cemetery, and the bride died of a broken heart. Read right here if you don't believe it!"

"But I'm the bridegroom myself!"

"And you went to the next world? Tell me about it!"

But the young man turned deathly pale, sank to the ground, and died before he could tell one single thing he had seen.

1. Meaning from Context: Fill in the blanks with the appropriate word from the list given below. When necessary, refer to the story to help determine meaning. The numbers in parentheses in this exercise and all that follow refer to the section in the story where the word appears.

harp, gazing, survivors, cottage, grave, cemetery, foliage, yawned, bass, crumbling

1. Almost everyone in the plane crash died. There were only two

   _____ . (2)

2. The widow visited her husband's _____ on the anniversary of his death. (2)

3. It looked as if the earth _____ because there was such a wide opening in the ground. (2)

4. A _____ is a stringed musical instrument that can stand by itself. (5)

5. The _____ is another musical instrument with strings, but it is not freestanding. (5)

6. We went out to the country to see the autumn _____ , but last night's storm had left the trees bare. (5)

7. The teacher told the student that instead of _____ out the window, he should be looking at his book. (5)

8. It is interesting to read the inscriptions on graves in an old

_____ . (7)

9. She only lived in a small_____ , but she daydreamed about living in a palace. (7)

10. We visited an ancient temple that once had been magnificent but now was

a _____ ruin. (9)

2. Synonyms: Replace the underlined word or words with the correct synonym. Choose from the following list:

witnessed, hereafter, assure, pledged, nerve, gaped, displayed, embraced, splendor, packed, very, account, thumbed, started, deadly

1. The bride and bridgegroom <u>made a promise</u> to always love each other. (1)
2. He had <u>observed</u> much of the fighting during the Civil War. (3)
3. It requires a great deal of <u>courage</u> to be a race car driver. (3)
4. The soldier <u>hugged</u> his girlfriend before leaving on the train. (4)
5. Not everyone believes in an <u>afterlife</u>. (4)
6. On his first visit to New York, he <u>stared</u> at all the sights. (5)
7. The <u>magnificence</u> of Paradise was breathtaking. (5)
8. All their works of art are <u>exhibited</u> in one room. (5)
9. She <u>jumped</u> when she heard the loud, unexpected noise. (6)
10. They <u>crammed</u> all the people into the small room. (7)
11. I can <u>convince</u> you that the statement is true. (8)
12. We found it difficult to believe his <u>report</u> of the incident. (8)
13. He <u>scanned</u> rapidly through the book. (9)
14. The police want to know the <u>exact</u> day he disappeared. (9)
15. It was a <u>deathly</u> dull evening. (9)

3. Antonyms: Choose the word in parentheses that completes each sentence appropriately.

1. It was a (joyously/drearily) beautiful day.
2. Although she had never taken dancing lessons, she danced (gracefully/clumsily).
3. The sun (vanished/appeared) from behind the clouds.
4. After being in the dark for so long, he was blinded by the (pale/ brilliant) light of the sun.
5. He is a man of (multiple/single) interests.

6. Although they are friends, they don't seem very (aloof/close).

7. Since her taste is (simple/elaborate), she wouldn't buy such a fancy dress.

4. Idioms and Special Expressions: Circle the letter in front of the answer that has the same meaning as the expression quoted from the story.

1. "Very well, suit yourself." (6)
   a. Buy yourself a suit.
   b. Put your suit on.
   c. Do what you want.

2. "Where on earth am I?" (7)
   a. What part of the world is this?
   b. Where could I possibly be?
   c. Am I on earth?

3. "I don't recognize it for the life of me." (8)
   a. I'd give up my life to recognize it.
   b. Because of my life I don't recognize it.
   c. No matter how hard I try, I'm unable to recognize it.

4. "He took heart." (4)
   a. He let his emotions guide him.
   b. He got his courage up.
   c. He felt his heart.

5. "Goodness knows!" (5)
   a. Only someone good knows.
   b. It is impossible to know.
   c. It is good to know.

6. "Before you knew it." (4)
   a. in the twinkling of an eye
   b. before anyone else knew it
   c. after a long time

7. "This is a ticklish situation." (2)
   a. The situation causes tickling.
   b. The situation is laughable.
   c. The situation needs to be handled carefully.

8. "It will then be up to him." (2)
   a. He will be able to come up.
   b. He will have to decide.
   c. He will have to come.

9. "The bride died of a broken heart." (9)
   a. She died of a heart attack.
   b. She died of sorrow.
   c. She died from an accident that injured her heart.

5A. Word Formation: When necessary, look for where the words given in the table on page 154 occur in the story. Try to determine meaning from context.

5B. Complete the following sentences with the correct form of the given word.

1. The news story was based only on _____ .   *supposed*

2. _____ an airplane crash is unlikely.   *survive*

3. It is not _____ to drive during a snowstorm.   *advice*

4. It is a _____ problem.   *worry*

5. The town had changed beyond _____ .   *recognize*

6. He couldn't remember what he had _____ .   *dream*

7. We had a _____ together.   *chatter*

8. He needs a great deal of _____ in his new job.   *guide*

9. The room was painted a _____ blue.   *paleness*

9. Did you sign your letter "Sincerely" or   *affection*
   "_____"?

6. Two-Word Verbs: Insert the adverbial particle that best completes each sentence in the blank provided.

1. Is it all right to call _____ someone without first calling them up on the telephone? (2)

2. Did you find _____ how much it costs? (4)

3. You can turn _____ anytime you get tired. (3)

4. Come _____ ! We will be late if we don't leave right now. (5)

5. Won't you come _____ with me? (4)

6. Move _____ ! You are holding up the traffic. (5)

7. I can show her how to do it, but it is _____ to her to get it done. (2)

8. If you don't watch out, you may end _____ getting hurt. (2)

9. What time do you normally wake _____ ? (5)

PARTICIPLE	NOUN	VERB	ADJECTIVE	ADVERB
supposed (2) supposing	supposition	suppose	supposable	supposedly
survived surviving	survival survivor (2)	survive		
advised advising	advice (2) adviser advisability	advise	advisable unadvisable advisory	advisably
guided guiding (5)	guide guidance	guide		
worried (6) worrying	worry worrier	worry	worrisome	worrisomely
recognized recognizing	recognition	recognize (7)	recognizable unrecognizable	recognizably
paled paling	paleness	pale	pale (9)	palely
affected affecting	affection (1) affectation	affect	affectionate	affectionately
dreamed dreaming (8)	dream dreamer	dream	dreamy dreamlike	dreamily
chatted chatting	chat chatter	chat (4)	chatty	

7. Structure: Verbs with infinitive objects.

SUBJECT	VERB	INFINITIVE	OBJECT
He	was planning	to get	married.

Certain verbs may take an infinitive object. The verbs in the sentence above may take an infinitive object but not a gerund (-ing form) object. The infinitive object of this type of verb never has a subject. The following is a partial list of verbs in this category:

agree	fail	neglect
attempt	forget	offer
begin	hesitate	plan
care	hope	prefer
continue	intend	pretend
decide	learn	promise
desire	long	refuse
try	mean	remember
		start

7A. Write ten sentences using different verbs from the above list. Use an infinitive object in each sentence.

Example: We agreed to come.

SUBJECT	VERB	OBJECT	
		subject	infinitive
If you	want		to find out ...
If you	want	them	to find out ...

The verbs in the sentences above may take an infinitive object with or without a subject. If the subject is a pronoun, it is in the objective form. They also do not take a gerund object. The following is a partial list of verbs of this type:

like	ask	need
prepare	expect	want
would like		

7B. Write ten sentences using five different verbs from the above list. In one sentence, use the verb with an infinitive object without a subject. In the next sentence, use the same verb with an infinitive object that has a subject.

Example: I expect to be on time.

I expect him to be on time.

8. Reading Comprehension: Circle the letter in front of the phrase that best completes each sentence.

1. The bridegroom went to the priest because
   a. he wanted to get married.
   b. he didn't know how to keep his promise.
   c. his friend had died.
2. The friend came back from the dead because
   a. he wanted to be at the wedding.
   b. he didn't want to be punished for breaking his promise.
   c. he was tired of being in Purgatory.
3. The bridegroom did not want to go all the way to the cemetery because
   a. he was getting married that night.
   b. he was afraid of cemeteries.
   c. he wanted to be with his wife on the first night of their marriage.
4. While in Paradise the bridegroom
   a. fell asleep.
   b. found it difficult to tear himself away from each spot he visited.
   c. urged the dead man to show him more.
5. "Enough? If I had my choice . . ."
   In the above quote, it is understood that the bridegroom's choice would be
   a. to return to earth.
   b. to stay longer.
   c. not to see any more since he has had enough.
6. The bridegroom didn't recognize the cemetery because
   a. it had become crowded because many more people had been buried there.
   b. it was no longer a cemetery.
   c. it was a different cemetery.
7. The bridegroom left
   a. in the sixteenth century and returned in the nineteenth.
   b. in the nineteenth century and returned in the twentieth.
   c. in the seventeenth century and returned in the twentieth.

8. The bride died
   a. when she was an old woman.
   b. not too long after the bridegroom disappeared.
   c. the same time as the bridegroom.
9. The sacristan
   a. believed the bridegroom's story.
   b. thought the bridegroom was imagining things.
   c. had never heard of such a story.
10. The bishop
    a. had never heard of the story.
    b. did not believe the story.
    c. had been told the story as a child.

9A. Controlled Writing Practice: Write nine sentences using the two-word verbs from Exercise 6. Model your sentences on those used in Exercise 6 and those used in the story.

9B. Write a summary of the story. Use the following sentence as your beginning sentence:

"Not wanting to break a promise that had been made between them, the young man went to his dead friend's grave to ask him to be his best man."

9C. Change the following sentences from direct speech to reported speech.

1. "This is a ticklish situation," said the priest.

   _____

   _____

2. "I really can't say," answered the dead man.

   _____

   _____

3. "You're dreaming," said the old man.

   _____

   _____

4. The youth said, "The time has come for you to be my best man."

   _____

   _____

5. His friend answered, "I understand. You can turn back any time you like."

   _____

   _____

10. Topics for Discussion and Writing

      A. Compare and contrast the bridegroom with Tu Thuc in "The Search for the Land of Bliss."

      B. "I didn't expect to see him tied to the world of dust and sorrow." Giang Huong's mother said this with regard to Tu Thuc. Does this also apply to the bridegroom? If so, explain how it applies.

      C. The idea of leaving this world for a short time and returning to find that many years have passed is found in folk stories all over the world. From the other stories we have read, we can also see other universal themes. What do you think is the explanation for so many similar stories turning up in so many different places?

Master List of Words in Vocabulary Exercises*

abandoned (5)
absence (7)
absorbed (7)
accepted (8)
accomplish (12)
accounts (6)
actually (8)
additional (13)
adhered (6)
adopted (6)
advanced (4)
afar (5)
aid (6)
alarming (6)
alighted (11)
allowed (2)
alms (11)
aloof (8)
alter (5)
amazed (1)
ancient (11)
anguished (1)
appalled (5)
appeared (9)
approaching (10)
approval (12)
approximate (5)
ascending (10)
ascertain (7)
assembled (9)
assured (10)
astonished (2)
astrologer (5)
attract (7)
autumn (13)

bade (10)

banquet (7)
bared (8)
barren (10)
base (13)
bass (14)
bed (11)
beheld (10)
benevolence (1)
bit of (3)
blinding (21)
bliss (7)
boldly (6)
breakneck (8)
breeze (9)
brief (10)
brilliant (12)
bulging (9)

cackle (9)
case (3)
cast (12)
ceased (4)
cemetery (14)
chamber (3)
characters (7)
clad (12)
cloak (2)
close (3)
cluster (7)
commanded (9)
commotion (8)
companions (2)
compassion (12)
compensation (13)
complexion (10)
conclave (12)
confident (1)

conical (13)
conjugal (7)
conjunction (5)
conscious (6)
consented (9)
consider (10)
consolation (10)
constructed (10)
consult (5)
consultation (12)
consume (12)
converted (12)
corrupt (4)
cottage (14)
countenances (12)
cowardly (6)
craft (3)
crazy (4)
creature (4)
critically (10)
crouched (6)
crowd (2)
crude (12)
crumbling (14)
cultivation (7)
curing (2)

daunted (6)
dawn (4)
deadly (14)
dearly (1)
debris (3)
deck (4)
declared (13)
declined (11)
deep (7)
delayed (10)

*Numbers in parentheses refer to the story in which the word is first used in an exercise.

delighted (8)
deliverance (6)
deluge (9)
denied (2)
depart (7)
depressed (10)
descended (9)
desolate (10)
destiny (5)
destroyed (10)
determined (11)
devastate (3)
dew (12)
dilapidated (13)
dim (9)
disappeared (10)
disciples (13)
discourage (9)
discovered (2)
disguised (11)
disintegrated (12)
displayed (14)
dispute (8)
distant (3)
distressed (1)
doomed (8)
downpour (4)
dreadful (5)

elapsed (3)
embraced (7)
emerged (12)
encountered (8)
enraged (9)
erected (7)
essential (1)
evil (4)
exceptional (7)
excluded (9)
excursion (13)
exhausted (3)
exhorted (11)
expands (13)
exterior (5)

fails (6)
faintly (7)
faith (2)
faithful (9)
fast (11)
fasten (3)

fine (12)
fled (5)
flocked (7)
foliage (14)
folk (3)
fond of (3)
forebears (13)
foreground (12)
foresaken (7)
fragment (7)
fraternal (7)
fresh (3)
fringe (2)
fruitful (4)
fulfill (7)
furious (8)
further (2)

gaped (14)
gathered (11)
gaze (12)
generosity (3)
gentle (9)
gnarled (9)
gracefully (14)
graciously (1)
grasped (3)
gravely (1)
gravity (1)
greeted (1)
grew (11)
grief (7)
groped (13)

harassed (6)
hardly (4)
hardships (9)
harp (10)
harvest (4)
hatchet (5)
headdresses (12)
health (2)
heap (11)
heavily (3)
heedless (4)
hell (9)
hemorrhage (2)
hereafter (14)
hide (12)
hindrance (6)
homeliness (12)

honorable (9)
host (10)
howled (3)
huge (3)
humbly (1)

ignorant (6)
immortal (13)
immortality (9)
implored (12)
incapable (5)
incredulous (10)
indicated (10)
indifferent (13)
inevitable (5)
inexplicable (13)
injected (3)
innumerable (1)
inquired (11)
inquiringly (12)
insanity (8)
intense (1)
invigorating (7)
invoked (13)

jackal (11)
jeered (4)
joyously (14)

lad (6)
lapping (4)
launched (12)
leafed (10)
leisure (13)
lightly (3)
live (11)
living beings (9)
loaded (4)
locks (5)
lulled (9)

maiden (8)
man (6)
mango (11)
marriage (7)
marvel (7)
mass (9)
mate (4)
molested (6)
mortified (6)
mossy (13)
mound (10)

mourn (2)
multiple (14)
multiplied (4)

nape (5)
native (10)
nearby (12)
neglect (7)
nerve (14)
normal (1)
numerous (1)

observed (5)
obsessed (5)
obvious (12)
offerings (9)
often (7)
ordeal (12)
order (2)
otter (11)
overjoyed (8)

packed (14)
palace (3)
pale (12)
pardon (8)
parentage (6)
penance (12)
pensive (8)
peony (13)
perceived (11)
period (12)
perish (3)
picturesque (13)
pious (7)
pitch (4)
plain (10)
pleaded (2)
pledged (14)
plucked (4)
poison (3)
pondered (7)
positive (7)
post house (8)
poverty (12)
preaching (11)
precious (12)
precise (5)
presented (7)
pressed (2)
priceless (13)

proclaimed (11)
prophecy (3)
protectress (10)
provisions (3)
pulp (8)

radiant (13)
raft (3)
rage (6)
reach (8)
realm (9)
reared (8)
receded (4)
recite (13)
reckoned (13)
recounted (7)
reflected (9), (11)
released (13)
remained (4)
repaid (3)
reported (3)
reproaches (13)
rescued (9)
resembled (5)
resigned (1)
responded (1)
restore (1)
rctained (7)
returned (11)
reveal (8)
revolted (5)
righteous (4)
rioting (4)
rosy (4)
route (10)
ruddy (8)
rustle (9)

sacred (9)
sanity (8)
scrubbed (9)
search (1)
seeking (11)
seldom (7)
selected (12)
serene (10)
severity (1)
sheaves (12)
shifting (13)
shock (10)
shrine (9)

sign (4)
simple (5)
sipped (13)
sites (13)
skiff (13)
sleek (5)
slew (6)
somber (12)
sought (9)
sound (8)
soundly (8)
spanning (13)
special (1)
spies (12)
splendor (14)
spoiled (3)
sprang (8)
squeezing (11)
staff (6)
started (14)
startled (12)
steadfast (5)
steep (13)
stinginess (3)
strained (8)
stranger (1)
strike (3)
strum (13)
stunted (10)
sturdy (4)
stutter (8)
subjugated (12)
submerged (3)
succeeds (6)
summit (5)
supplications (9)
supreme (12)
surface (3)
survivors (3)

tangled (9)
tender (11)
tenderness (1)
termination (6)
terrified (10)
terror (12)
throne (9)
throngs (8)
thumbed (14)
tightly (12)

tiny (3)
took place (11)
tortured (9)
touching (5)
trail (10)
transformed (7)
tremble (2)
trials (12)
triumph (8)
trouble (2)
twine (7)

unconcerned (13)
unconvinced (10)
underworld (9)

unsheathed (8)
upward (5)
useful (3)
useless (11)

vanished (8)
vast (13)
verse (13)
very (14)
virtues (11)

warned (5)
watertight (4)
wealth (12)

weary (8)
weeping (2)
well known (1)
wickedness (4)
wise (11)
withdrew (12)
withered (7)
witnessed (7)
worried (6)
wretched (6)
writhed (3)

yawned (14)

Master List of Words in Word Formation Tables

accept (3)
accomplish (12)
adhere (6)
administrate (13)
adopt (5)
advise (14)
affect (14)
afflict (6)
agree (3)
allow (2)
answer (11)
approach (10)
approve (12)
assure (10)
astonish (2)
attend (6)
attract (13)

believe (2)
breathe (8)
brilliance (10)

celebrate (13)
chat (14)
collect (12)
comment (8)
condition (6)
confide (1)
console (7)
consult (5)

continue (4)
corrupt (4)
counsel (7)
crazy (4)
create (4)
creep (7)

decide (3)
dedicate (10)
deliver (6)
deny (2)
depart (11)
destine (5)
destroy (4)
determine (11)
devastate (3)
devote (7)
disguise (11)
disintegrate (12)
distress (1)
dream (14)

empower (2)
enchant (13)
encourage (12)
endanger (6)
endure (7)
enlighten (13)
entertain (8)
except (7)

explain (13)
explore (13)

faith (2)
fear (2)
force (9)
forget (4)
forgive (8)
freshen (4)

generosity (11)
gratify (6)
guide (14)

hesitate (13)
hope (9)
horrify (6)

imagine (8)
immortalize (9)
implore (12)
inscribe (7)
insist (8)
inspire (13)
intensify (1)
invite (8)
isolate (5)

kindness (10)

laugh (2)
live (11)

manage (5)
marry (1)
miraculous (10)
mistake (10)
mourn (2)
multiply (4)

neglect (7)
number (1)

obey (10)
observe (5)
occasion (3)
offer (11)
officiate (2)
oppose (13)
originate (5)

pale (14)
perceive (11)
perfect (9)

persuade (8)
possess (8)
precision (5)
prepare (3)
produce (7)
promise (4)
prophesy (3)
protect (3)
punish (9)

question (1)

radiate (12)
reflect (11)
remark (8)
respond (1)
restore (1)

sacrifice (12)
save (4)
search (1)

seek (9)
submerged (3)
succeed (6)
suffer (2)
suppose (14)
survive (14)

tangle (9)
terminate (6)
terrorize (12)
transform (7)
tremble (2)

use (9)

virtue (11)

watch (3)
withdraw (12)
worry (14)

Master List of Two-Word Verbs

bear up (4)
be out (9)
be up (14)
blot out (4)
bring back (9)
bring in (3)

call on (14)
carry away (3)
come along (14)
come back (4)
come on (14)
come out (8)
cut off (8)

end up (14)

find out (14)

gather up (10)

go away (9)
go back (3)
go down (3)
go off (3)

happen by (8)

look back (9)
look out (8)
look up (10)

move on (14)

pick up (8)
put in (8)
put out (9)

run off (3)

run out (8)

send away (10)
set off (10)
set out (8)
start off (10)
stay on (8)
store up (4)

throw back (3)
turn back (9)

wake up (14)
wander about (9)
went on (4)
went up (10)

Master List of Word plus Preposition or Preposition plus Word Combinations

acquainted with (10)
at that moment (2)
attracted to (12)

beyond repair (12)
by boat (13)
by chance (13)

confided to (13)
converted into (12)

dedicated to (10)
distracted by (5)
deep into (5)
dressed in (12)

filled with (12)

guilty of (10)

healed of (10)

incapable of (5)

in search of (1)
in shame (12)
interested in (13)

known for (1)
know of (1)

laugh at (2)
laugh with (2)
listen to (10)
look for (1)

mourn for (2)

on the verge of (5)
overcome with (12)

pass through (12)
pity on (1)
ponder over (10)
possessed of (10)
presented to (12)

proof of (10)

resigned to (1)

shocked at (13)
succeed in (13)
suffer from (2)

take advantage of (5)
take into (5)
take pity on (5)
toward evening (5)

unconcerned about (13)

wait for (5)
walk toward (12)
weep for (2)
wish for (13)
withdrew from (12)
worthy of (13)

Bibliography

ALLEN, W.S., gen. ed, *Longman Structural Readers*. London: Longman, n.d.

CLARKE, MARK, AND SANDRA SILBERSTEIN, "Toward a Realization of Psycholinguistic Principles in the ESL Reading Class," in *Reading in a Second Language*, eds. Ronald Mackay, Bruce Barkman, R.R. Jordan. Rowley, Mass.: Newbury House, 1979.

GOODMAN, KENNETH, "Words and Morphemes in Reading," in *Psycholinguistics and the Teaching of Reading*, eds. Kenneth Goodman and James Fleming. Newark, Del.: International Reading Association, 1969.

_____, "Psycholinguistic Universals in the Reading Process," in *The Psychology of Second Language Learning*, eds. Paul Pimsleur and Terrence Quinn. Cambridge: University Press, 1971.

_____, "Analysis of Oral Reading Miscues: Applied Psycholinguistics," in *Psycholinguistics and Reading*, ed. Frank Smith. New York: Holt, Rinehart and Winston, 1979.

KEYES, CHARLES, *Southeast Asian Reseach Tools: Cambodia*. Honolulu: Asian Studies Program, University of Hawaii, 1979.

_____, *Southeast Asian Research Tools: Laos*. Honolulu: Asian Studies Program, University of Hawaii, 1979.

KOLERS, PAUL, "Reading is Only Incidentally Visual," in *Psycholinguistics and the Teaching of Reading*, eds. Kenneth Goodman and James Fleming. Newark, Del.: International Reading Association, 1969.

LEFEVRE, CARL, *Linguistics and the Teaching of Reading*. New York: McGraw-Hill, 1962.

MACKAY, RONALD, BRUCE BARKMAN, and R. R. JORDAN, eds., *Reading in a Second Language*. Rowley, Mass.: Newbury House, 1979.

MILNE, JOHN, gen. ed, *Heinemann Guided Readers*. London: Heinemann Educational Books, n.d.

MUNBY, JOHN, "Teaching Intensive Reading Skills," in *Reading in a Second Language*, eds. Ronald Mackay, Bruce Barkman, R. R. Jordan. Rowley, Mass.: Newbury House, 1979.

NATIONAL INDOCHINESE CLEARING HOUSE, *Vietnamese History, Literature, and Folklore*. Intermediate/Secondary Education Series, No. 1. *Indochinese Refugee Education Guides*. Washington, D.C.: Center for Applied Linguistics, 1975.

PAULSTON, CHRISTINA, AND MARY BRUDER, *Teaching English as a Second Language: Techniques and Procedures*. Cambridge, Mass.: Winthrop, 1976.

RIVERS, WILGA, *Teaching Foreign Language Skills*. Chicago: University of Chicago Press, 1968.

————, "Language Learning and Language Teaching," in *Second Language Acquisition Research*, ed. William Ritchie. New York: Academic Press, 1978.

RODRIGUEZ, RICHARD, "A Memoir of a Bilingual Childhood," *The American Scholar*, Winter 1980—1981.

SCHUMANN, JOHN, "Implications of Pidginization and Creolization for the Study of Adult Second Language Acquisition," in *New Frontiers in Second Language Learning*, eds. John Schumann and Nancy Stenson. Rowley, Mass.: Newbury House, 1974.

————, *The Pidginization Process: A Model for Second Language Acquisition*. Rowley, Mass.: Newbury House, 1978.

SMITH, FRANK, *Understanding Reading: A Psycholinguistic Analysis of Reading and Learning to Read*. New York: Holt, Rinehart and Winston, 1971.

————, ed. *Psycholinguistics and Reading*. New York: Holt, Rinehart and Winston, 1973.

Answer Key for Vocabulary and Reading Comprehension Exercises

1. The Mustard Seed

Exercise 1: a

Exercise 2

1. restore	2. essential	3. benevolence
4. anguished	5. responded	6. distressed
7. gravity	8. graciously	9. greeted
10. special	11. numerous	12. dearly

Exercise 3

1. humbly	2. innumerable	3. well known
4. insecure	5. resigned	6. severity
7. intense	8. normal	

Exercise 4

1. c	2. a	3. c
4. b	5. c	6. a

Exercise 5B

1. distressed	2. questionnaire	3: responsive
4. restore	5. numerous	6. intensely
7. confidential	8. searched	9. marriagable

Exercise 6

1. of	2. for	3. for
4. of	5. to	6. on

Exercise 8

1. F	2. F	3. F
4. T	5. F	6. F
7. T	8. T	9. F

2. The Daughter of Jairus

Exercise 1

1. crowded
2. hemorrhage
3. companions
4. curing
5. denied
6. mourn
7. fringe
8. allowed
9. cloak
10. order

Exercise 2

1. pleaded with
2. discovered
3. trouble
4. tremble
5. weeping
6. stifling
7. astonished
8. further
9. faith
10. crowd

Exercise 3

1. deny
2. rejoice
3. discovered
4. forbidden
5. deteriorated
6. health

Exercise 4B

1. trembled
2. astonishment
3. faith
4. mourners
5. denied
6. laugh
7. allowed
8. powerless
9. insufferable
10. official

Exercise 5

1. for
2. at
3. from
4. for
5. from
6. at
7. in

Exercise 7

1. b
2. c
3. b
4. a
5. b
6. c
7. a
8. a
9. a
10. b

3. The Golden Turtle

Exercise 1

1. tended
2. prophecy
3. devastate
4. raft
5. provisions
6. submerged
7. surface
8. perish
9. survivors
10. repaid
11. injected
12. palace
13. chamber

Exercise 2

1. a bit of	2. fond of	3. spoiled
4. debris	5. fasten	6. grasped
7. exhausted	8. howled	9. elapsed
10. writhed	11. reported	12. folk
13. strike	14. craft	15. case

Exercise 3

1. afloat	2. generosity	3. distant
4. useless	5. an antidote	6. lightly
7. huge		

Exercise 4B

1. submerged	2. protective	3. occasionally
4. prepared	5. prophesied	6. devastation
7. decision	8. watchful	9. agreeable
10. accepted		

Exercise 6

1. b	2. b	3. a
4. b	5. b	6. c
7. c	8. a	9. b

4. The Great Flood

Exercise 1

1. rioting	2. pitch	3. watertight
4. deck	5. mate	6. jeered
7. loaded	8. downpour	9. rosy
10. lapping	11. harvest	12. fruitful

Exercise 2

1. multiplied	2. corrupt	3. hardly
4. righteous	5. heedless	6. plucked
7. receded	8. ceased	9. wickedness
10. creature	11. sign	

Exercise 3

1. evil	2. decrepit	3. advanced
4. dawn	5. crazy	6. stale
7. departed		

Exercise 4B

1. continuation	2. multitude	3. forgetfulness
4. freshly	5. promise	6. craziness

7. corrupt   8. destructive   9. creative
10. saved

Exercise 5

1. out   2. up   3. on
4. up   5. down   6. back

Exercise 6

1. c   2. a   3. b
4. b   5. a   6. b
7. c   8. a   9. b
10. b

5. The Mountain of Hope

Exercise 1

1. summit   2. resembled   3. nape
4. inevitable   5. touching   6. locks
7. consult   8. dreadful   9. abandoned
10. appalled   11. astrologer   12. conjunction
13. steadfast

Exercise 2

1. alter   2. sleek   3. fled
4. destiny   5. afar   6. dreadful
7. revolted   8. observed   9. erect
10. obsessed   11. hatchet   12. precise

Exercise 3

1. upward   2. inevitable   3. precise
4. precise   5. capable   6 interior

Exercise 4

1. b   2. b   3. b
4. a

Exercise 5B

1. manager   2. originally   3. explanation
4. destination   5. isolation   6. distractions
7. adoptable   8. consultation   9. precisely
10. observant

Exercise 6

1. toward
4. of
7. of

2. by
5. of
8. for

3. into
6. on

Exercise 7

1. c
4. b
7. a

2. a
5. a
8. a

3. b
6. b
9. a

6. The Story of Oedipus

Exercise 1

1. warned
4. molested
7. staff
10. adhered

2. adopted
5. crouched
8. deliverance

3. slew
6. boldly
9. parentage

Exercise 2

1. rage
4. harassed
7. mortified
10. termination

2. prophecy
5. accounts
8. perished
11. aid

3. daunted
6. alarming
9. wretched

Exercise 3

1. lad
4. cowardlv
7. conscious

2. inhibit
5. abandoned
8. a hinderance

3. retreated
6. succeeds

Exercise 4 (Answers may vary.)

1. threw, died
3. killed herself

2. was discovered
4. died

Exercise 5

1. conditional
4. grateful
7. horror
10. affliction

2. endangered
5. successful
8. adheres

3. attendant
6. terminal
9. deliverer

Exercise 7

1. c
4. b
7. c
10. c

2. c
5. c
8. b

3. b
6. b
9. b

7. The Seed of Good Conversation

Exercise 1

1. banquet
4. twine
7. marvel
10. conjugal

2. presented
5. erected
8. cultivation
11. faintly

3. cluster
6. withered
9. fraternal

Exercise 2

1. deep
4. bliss
7. grief
10. retained
13. ascertain
16. marriage

2. fulfill
5. pondered
8. characters
11. flocked
14. fragment

3. forsaken
6. embraced
9. exceptional
12. recounted to
15. invigorating

Exercise 3

1. transformed
4. deep
7. absence
10. pious

2. seldom
5. depart
8. neglect

3. positive
6. absorbed
9. attract

Exercise 4

1. k
2. i
3. g
4. d
5. a
6. c

7. e
8. f
9. b
10. h
11. j

Exercise 5B

1. neglected
4. endure
7. transformation

2. devoted
5. creepy
8. inscription

3. product
6. counselor
9. exceptionally

Exercise 7

1. b
4. c
7. a
10. c
13. c

2. b
5. a
8. b
11. b
14. b

3. b
6. b
9. b
12. a

8. Pome and Peel

Exercise 1

1. F	2. F	3. T	4. F
5. F	6. F	7. T	8. F
9. F	10. F		

Exercise 2

1. ruddy	2. pulp	3. post house
4. unsheathed	5. chamber	6. vanished
7. doomed	8. strained	9. stuttered
10. breakneck	11. throngs	

Exercise 3

1. reared	2. soundly	3. actually
4. reached	5. crazy	6. dispute
7. pensive	8. bared	9. commotion
10. pardon	11. sprang	12. sound
13. weary	14. furious	15. encountered

Exercise 4

1. overjoyed	2. conceal	3. aloof
4. triumph	5. crazy	6. rejected
7. appalled		

Exercise 5

1. i	2. g	3. f
4. d	5. c	6. b
7. a	8. e	9. h

Exercise 6B

1. possession	2. remarkably	3. breath
4. persuasive	5. comment	6. entertainer
7. insistent	8. imaginatively	9. Invited
10. forgiveness		

Exercise 7

1. off	2. out	3. up
4. on	5. by	6. out
7. out	8. out	9. in

Exercise 9

1. b	2. c	3. c

4. c   5. a   6. b
7. a   8. b   9. c
10. b   11. a

9. Gentle Gwan Yin

Exercise 1

1. faithful   2. reflected   3. scrubbed
4. tortured   5. cackle   6. Hell
7. realm   8. immortality   9. throne
10. mass   11. tangled   12. rustle
13. shrine   14. sacred   15. excluded

Exercise 2

1. living being   2. consented   3. hardships
4. deluge   5. supplications   6. rescued
7. the underworld   8. sought   9. bulging
10. gnarled   11. commanded   12. breeze
13. sacred   14. offerings   15. assembled

Exercise 3

1. dim   2. honorable   3. excluded
4. discourage   5. consented   6. descended
7. enrage   8. assemble   9. appeared
10. gentle

Exercise 4B

1. consent   2. assembly   3. sought
4. punishment   5. mortally   6. usable
7. perfectionist   8. force   9. tangle
10. hopeless

Exercise 4C

paragraph 1   the faithful, the childless
paragraph 2   the youngest, the sick, the poor

Exercise 5

1. back   2. back   3. away
4. out   5. back   6. away
7. about   8. out

Exercise 7

1. b   2. a   3. c
4. b   5. c   6. b
7. c   8. c   9. a

10. The Virgin of Guadalupe

Exercise 1

1. F
2. T
3. F
4. T
5. F
6. T
7. F
8. T
9. F
10. T

Exercise 2

1. subjugated
2. route
3. barren
4. stunted
5. host
6. beheld
7. assured
8. protectress
9. incredulous
10. Spies
11. critically
12. delayed
13. shock
14. complexion

Exercise 3

1. mound
2. desolate
3. startled
4. pondered over
5. brief
6. consider
7. reflected
8. approaching
9. miraculous
10. trail
11. serene
12. amazed
13. constructed
14. indicated
15. consolation

Exercise 4

1. native
2. forbade
3. disappeared
4. plain
5. elated
6. terrified
7. convinced
8. destroyed
9. exhilarated
10. subjugated

Exercise 5B

1. wondrously/ wonderfully
2. mistake
3. kind
4. protective
5. dedicate
6. brilliant
7. veneration
8. assurance
9. approach
10. disobedient

Exercise 6

1. up
2. over
3. to
4. away
5. up
6. of
7. of
8. off
9. of
10. with
11. up
12. off
13. of
14. to

Exercise 7

1. near the point of death

2. drew nearer
3. beyond all doubt
4. The news of the miracle spread rapidly.
5. took charge of the situation
6. from that day forward

Exercise 9

1. b	2. c	3. b
4. b	5. a	6. b
7. b	8. c	9. c
10. a		

11. The Hare-Mark on the Moon

Exercise 1

1. fast	2. preaching	3. mango
4. otter	5. heap	6. live
7. disguised	8. alighted	9. bed
10. inquired	11. jackals	12. squeezing

Exercise 2

1. exhorted	2. alms	3. reflected
4. determined	5. perceived	6. declined
7. seeking	8. took place	9. proclaimed
10. grew		

Exercise 3

1. vices	2. scattered	3. useless
4. wise	5. declined	6. tender
7. modern	8. forsook	

Exercise 4B

1. determination	2. reflection	3. answering
4. use	5. offered	6. perception
7. virtuously	8. departing	9. generously
10. lively		

Exercise 6

1. F	2. F	3. T
4. T	5. F	6. F
7. T	8. F	9. F
10. F	11. T	

12. The Sun and the Moon God

Exercise 1

1. T	2. T	3. F	4. T
5. T	6. T	7. F	8. T
9. F	10. T		

Exercise 2

1. conclave	2. converted	3. consume
4. consultation	5. penance	6. dew
7. precious	8. sheaves	9. additional
10. clad	11. hide	12. crude
13. headdresses	14. somber	15. trials
16. ordeal	17. disintegrated	18. launched
19. blinding	20. inquiringly	

Exercise 3

1. submerged	2. considered	3. conclave
4. selected	5. cast	6. emerged from
7. accomplish	8. obvious	9. terror
10. compassion	11. constructed	12. withdrew from
13. period	14. startled	15. countenances, somber
16. gaze	17. supreme	18. implored

Exercise 4

1. wealth	2. background	3. brief
4. homeliness	5. approval	6. pale
7. obvious	8. dispersed	9. withdrew from
10. worthless	11. fine	12. far away
13. tightly	14. attract	15. diminished

Exercise 5B

1. accomplishment	2. approvingly	3. collection
4. withdrawn	5. terrorist	6. implored
7. sacrifice	8. encouragement	9. disintegrated
10. radiantly		

Exercise 5C

Section 4   the young, the rich, the noble
Section 6   the weathly, the poor (the ugly, the pure are also possible)
Section 10   the humble
Section 13   the simple-hearted, the brave

Exercise 6

1. through
2. into, into
3. with
4. from
5. to
6. in
7. with
8. in
9. to
10. toward

Exercise 7A

lit, flames, leaped, blaze, roaring, crackling, subsided, sizzling

Exercise 7B

ceremony, holy, worship, penance, meditate, sacrifice, offering, ritual

Exercise 7C

fiery, rays, radiated, light, blinding brilliance, glow

Exercise 8

1. b
2. b
3. a
4. b
5. c
6. a
7. a
8. c
9. c
10. b

13. The Search for the Land of Bliss

Exercise 1

1. F
6. T
2. F
7. F
3. T
8. T
4. F
9. F
5. T
10. F

Exercise 2

1. recite
2. sipped
3. peony
4. compensation
5. skiff
6. expands
7. strum
8. verse
9. steep
10. mossy
11. groped
12. picturesque
13. reckoned
14. spanning
15. dilapidated
16. conical

Exercise 3

1. vast
2. autumn
3. declared
4. reported
5. reproaches
6. disciples
7. shifting
8. radiant
9. excursion
10. sites
11. priceless
12. invoked

Exercise 4

1. immortal
2. detained
3. descending
4. worried
5. inexplicable
6. lulled
7. forebears
8. leisure
9. indifferent
10. base

Exercise 5

1. b
2. c
3. g
4. e
5. a
6. d
7. f
8. h
9. k
10. i
11. j

Exercise 6B

1. familiarize
2. enlighten
3. explanation
4. enchanted
5. attractively
6. opposite
7. administrative
8. explore
9. celebrities
10. hesitate

Exercise 7

1. in
2. of
3. at
4. by
5. in
6. by
7. about
8. of
9. for
10. to
11. beyond
12. in

Exercise 8

1. c
2. b
3. c
4. a
5. b
6. a
7. b
8. a
9. c
10. b
11. b
12. b
13. a
14. b

14. One Night in Paradise

Exercise 1

1. survivors
2. grave
3. yawned
4. harp
5. bass
6. foliage
7. gazing
8. cemetery
9. cottage
10. crumbling

Exercise 2

1. pledged
2. witnessed
3. nerve
4. embraced
5. hereafter
6. gaped
7. splendor
8. displayed
9. started

10. packed   11. assure   12. account
13. thumbed   14. very   15. deadly

Exercise 3

1. joyously   2. gracefully   3. appeared
4. brilliant   5. multiple   6. close
7. simple

Exercise 4

1. c   2. b   3. c
4. b   5. b   6. a
7. c   8. b   9. b

Exercise 5B

1. supposition   2. surviving   3. advisable
4. worrisome   5. recognition   6. dreamed
7. chat   8. guidance   9. pale
10. Affectionately

Exercise 6

1. on   2. out   3. back
4. on   5. along   6. on
7. up   8. up   9. up

Exercise 8

1. b   2. b   3. c
4. b   5. b   6. a
7. c   8. b   9. b
10. c